E.F. WELLS

His Art, Life and Times

ANTHONY H. HULL

ALAN SUTTON

First published in the United Kingdom in 1990 by
Alan Sutton Publishing Ltd · Phoenix Mill · Far Thrupp · Stroud · Gloucestershire

First published in the United States of America in 1991 by
Alan Sutton Publishing Inc · Wolfeboro Falls · NH 03896-0848

British Library Cataloguing in Publication Data

Hull, Anthony H. *1923–*
    E.F. Wells : his art, life and times.
    1. English paintings. Wells, E.F. (Edward Francis) 1876–1952
    I. Title
    759.2

    ISBN 0-86299-757-7

Library of Congress Cataloging in Publication Data applied for

Jacket illustration: Self-portrait of the Artist (*c. 1936*)

Typesetting and origination by
Alan Sutton Publishing Limited.
Typeset in 11/12 Palatino.
Printed in Great Britain by
Dotesios Printers Limited.

CONTENTS

LIST OF ILLUSTRATIONS

Jacket: *Self-portrait of the Artist, c. 1936*

COLOUR PLATES

BLACK-AND-WHITE ILLUSTRATIONS

FAMILY TREE SHOWING THE CONNECTION BETWEEN THE WELLS AND PELLEW FAMILIES

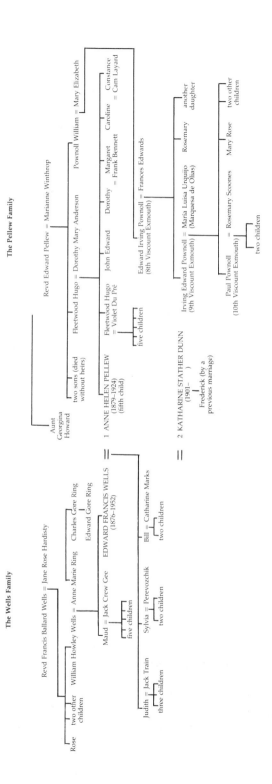

FOREWORD

This, the first book ever to be produced on the art and life of Edward Francis Wells (1876–1952), is but a small tribute to one who merits still greater attention. Well-known in his lifetime, he is now just beginning to be recognized as a major figure in the field of British watercolour painting, oil painting, and pastel portraiture.

A main purpose has been to present a cross-section of his work provided by the enclosed colour reproductions; but these represent the barest surface of his total output, which was prolific by any standards. In applying critical judgements here, the author has attempted a fair appraisal, but it is necessarily left to the viewer to judge for himself or herself what to make of this extraordinarily perceptive and sensitive artist from the material the author has chosen, or been able to present.

Within the tight limits for a book of this type, emphasis has been given in the text to Wells's efforts to attain fulfillment and perfection in his art. Trivia has thus been largely avoided, though trivia has to be reckoned with in any study of a lifetime. In other words, technique and other considerations of his professional life have been featured more than his personal life, at least where the latter has seemed irrelevant to his development as an artist.

Again because of various limits the provenance of many of his works has had to be omitted, though where his sitters are concerned as many as possible have been carefully researched for special mention. The same stringency regrettably applies to certain quotations from his letters and notes, as well as to press coverage. It would be a monumental task to fill all these gaps. Rather than undertake a task which might never be finished, it was felt wiser to proceed with what has been preserved and which can be kept to manageable proportions – all with a view to sustaining reader interest for one who is unquestionably a supremely gifted colourist and craftsman.

In studying the work of E.F. Wells one is reminded that the present age is one where representational realism is coming back into fashion after nearly a century of banishment. This has special meaning when it is considered that Edward's work is already part of the past, returning like a long lost ship, while much of later modern art has already been scuttled by both the public and critics themselves. His work moreover is eagerly being collected in Britain and elsewhere, in such diverse countries as Germany, Switzerland, Japan, and America.

The author is extremely indebted to the painter's surviving widow, Mrs K. Ormsby Wells. She has generously permitted the use of much material on which to construct this book. This includes access to her late husband's personal correspondence and her own recollections, not to mention the products of her efforts in giving frequent exhibitions of his work both during and after his lifetime. The artist's son William Wells, retired curator of the Burrell Collection in Glasgow, has also lent invaluable assistance in terms of scholarly sources. The same also applies to the artist's great niece Judith Wills in terms of genealogy. Outside the family circle, Mr Peter Scheiwe of Münster, Germany, in company with his wife Idalies, apart from being an avid E.F. Wells collector in his own right, has given inestimable help in furnishing many transparencies for reproduction in this book. Mrs Alice Gamble of Cheverells Mansion, Hertfordshire, along with her daughter Eleanor, both extended every form of courtesy to an author's request for assistance. And in the professional world at large Mr Nicholas Savage and staff of the Royal Academy Library, among other institutions, were extremely helpful in responding to all sorts of enquiry. To all of these can be added the author's own wife, Elizabeth, who patiently solved many difficulties in both language style and research which have considerably improved this book's preparation.

Last but not least are the many patrons who still remember Edward, and who at one time or another have expressed a willingness to furnish transparencies which are the lifeblood of this book. One such person is Mr Maurice Bowyer; Mrs Doris Bowyer is remembered for the lovely portrait by Edward which is herein reproduced. To these two, and to all his patrons and would-be collaborators, including those of the younger generation, the author wishes to express his deepest gratitude.

Sherborn, Massachusetts, USA
August 1990

CHAPTER ONE

EARLY YEARS

Edward Francis Wells was born in Calcutta, India, on 3 April 1876. His father, William Howley (pronounced 'Hooley') Wells, was an engineer who included among his accomplishments service as consultant in the planning and operation of the famous Clifton Suspension Bridge. He was also an inventor, devising, among other things, a new form of milk separator which went down well in the rural England of his day. But William Wells's professional life was concerned largely with India. Having joined the Indian Civil Service, he was subsequently posted to the offices of the municipal power house in Calcutta, and this explains the artist's birth in this city.

The artist's mother, born Annie Maria Ring, met William Howley in the early 1870s and some said it was love at first sight. At all events their son Edward was the apple of his parents' eyes, especially his mother's, while his father had a marked influence on Edward's later development. A daughter was also born, named Maud, who was to show great promise with the violin and creative writing.

Contrary to the myth, life was not all a bed of roses for English professional families living in India. Cholera was rife, for example, and Edward's parents had already lost two male infants from this dread disease. Indeed, its toll was heavy at the time; Theon Wilkinson's book on India, *Two Monsoons* tells of the graves of countless stricken babies who had died.[1] Edward's parents, afraid to continue living there, made the difficult decision to return to England. This meant that the father had to give up his prospects for a pension. Once home, however, William Howley renewed acquaintance with some of his Eton schoolfriends in his search for suitable employment. Among these was Lord Ilchester of Melbury Park in Dorset, who offered him the stewardship of his estates.

Thus it was at Evershot, the little village close to Melbury Park, not far from Yeovil, where Edward grew up and spent nearly twenty years of his life. When he first came to England at the age of three, the story goes that he uttered the Hindi word *Jow* to anyone walking in his path – his way of saying, 'Get out of my way!' He was quickly told that this wasn't done in England. Presumably the boy as quickly obeyed; and in fact he grew

Edward as a schoolboy, *c.* 1888

up rather reserved in his adopted country, at least in front of his elders.

This good behaviour was no doubt a product of his strict Victorian upbringing. His mother and father were both conforming members of the Church of England, and some of his relations were clergymen. His paternal grandfather, for example, the Reverend Francis Ballard Wells, was rector of Woodchurch in Kent, and William Howley Wells's godfather was, it is believed, the son of the Reverend William Howley (the Archbishop of Canterbury who informed the young Victoria that she was to be queen), which would account for his middle Christian name. Evidence suggests that Francis Ballard Wells served as secretary to the archbishop and this would explain the connection. But Ballard Wells also had a spell of bad luck. Whether he had a propensity for port or no, the story goes that while laid up with chronic gout at a time when the domestic servants had their day off, Ballard Wells was obliged to listen helplessly while a bunch of thieves in the next room made off with some family silver. Proof that villainy of this sort was as familiar in 1840 as it is today!

The boy was happy in this Christian atmosphere, though his idea of God later became far removed from the conventional God of his day. Every Sunday the little procession of father, mother, Edward, sister Maud, nurse Clara, and servants, walked the high street of Evershot to the local church. Lord Ilchester provided a beautiful secluded house in the village, known as 'Moorfields', for his steward, and church-going was an expected duty for the whole family. Everyone was contented in this setting. Among other delights, Moorfields was provided with a well-stocked greenhouse – peaches warm from the sun, grapes in white bloom. In later years Edward talked for hours about the house at Evershot.

The village as a whole was just as intriguing. The name Evershot comes from the Anglo-Saxon *Eofors-holt*, meaning a wild boar in the thicket (compare with the German words *Eber* and *Holz* meaning 'boar' and 'wood' respectively). Such a name obviously had something to do with the settlement's surroundings, tucked away as it is in the woods and under-growth of this cosy part of the Dorset hills. Close by, a spring still bubbles underground. Known as St John's Well, it provides a source to the River Frome that rises here before winding its picturesque course across Dorset to Poole Harbour and the sea. This well is situated near the local church of Evershot, mentioned above, which is known as St Osmond's. Developed probably in the reign of King Richard I ('the Lion-Heart'), the church still contains a late Norman font as well as part of a tower and chancel arches dating from this time. In the nineteenth century, however, the church was mainly rebuilt, with an enlarged chancel and a new south-facing aisle, along with a new tower. The bells were recast in 1775, now six in number, and bell-ringers thereafter summoned the worshippers with much gusto. Perhaps Edward in later years would have learnt that the rustic poet George Crabbe was rector here in the 1780s.

Edward would certainly have heard about the writer Thomas Hardy (1840–1928). The latter knew Evershot well and is said to have contributed to the design of Summer Lodge, reserved in the village for the heir to the Ilchester estates. Hardy's mother came from Melbury Osmond, the next village, and his parents were married there in the local church. It was in the cottage by Evershot Church, now known as 'Tess Cottage' that Hardy's famous character Tess had breakfast on her way to 'Emminster' (Beaminster). More tragically, it was in Evershot on her return that she was spotted by her fatal seducer, Alec d'Urberville.

As a child, Edward's values were of a simple order. There was the immense excitement at being given half a sovereign by an uncle; and though the family's style of living was rich in creature comforts – cygnet stuffed with rump steak was a casual dinner, syllabub an ordinary everyday pudding – his conduct was strictly vetted by his father. Standards, after all, had to be maintained; his father's job demanded it. A privilege of that era, incidentally, was the custom of telling railway staff where to stop your train. In Edward's case it would be Evershot station, a mile or so from the village (the railway line from Yeovil to Dorchester having long since disappeared); and there Edward could be seen alighting on the platform with his bag and baggage.

The family servants included a cook, parlour-maid, housemaid, and gardener, the usual staff of those times. Years later in the 1970s, a daughter of one of the family cooks was located in Evershot, living near to Moorfields. A lovable old lady, she well remembered 'Master Eddie' whenever he used to visit Evershot. 'He was happy and friendly, Master Eddie was,' she recalled, 'always walking the lanes with a pocket sketching-book at hand. He walked in haste, like, as if wanting to get there fast. And he had dark shining hair.' Her face beaming, remembering when she herself was barely ten years old as she caught sight of Edward, she reflected the rural spirit that still hung about the place then, uniting simple cottager with the Grand Master of the Foxhounds at Melbury. This rural, almost feudal, air has its landmarks. A mile or so from the village is a bridge with a grim warning to the effect that anyone convicted of damaging it is liable to the penalty of transportation – presumably to Australia!

At the age of nine Edward was sent to Sawgeen, a preparatory boarding-school in Bournemouth. Here he won prizes for scripture and science. Then at thirteen, he entered Clifton Public School. In later years he was generally reticent about his education. Explaining this, possibly, was his dislike of certain of its features, though he remained loyal to his old school as an institution. 'Keep your pecker up,' was the advice intoned by his father on Edward's return to Clifton after the holidays. The incessant farewells from his family would be followed by the herding together of sensitive (and insensitive) boys, the stern discipline, the inevitable bullying. But Edward apparently mastered the system. His schoolwork turned out average, but he excelled in sport, including the new game of tennis, and he became captain of his cricket team. A sure sign that he had won his spurs.

It was doubtless with some pride that he gazed upon his father's own spurs in the shape of the many gold-leaved prize books his father had won at Eton years before. But Edward was no bookworm; and in the early 1890s, as a schoolboy still, he declared his intention of becoming an artist. It is difficult to say what motivated his decision. Probably it was a mixture of a fast eye, plenty of local colour, and heredity, in which perhaps the spatial interests of his father and the detailed observations of his mother were translated in his mind into shape and colour. There was also an aunt who inspired him with her painting. In any event Edward had ample opportunity in the sleepy Dorset uplands to realize his dreams. It was both a lure and a challenge.

For this purpose he was given a studio by his father on his leaving Clifton, a tiny converted dairy at the side of Moorfields. Here Edward began to paint his first serious pictures. They were mostly landscapes of Evershot and surrounding villages. But he experimented with figures as well; and among his early work is a self-portrait done at the age of seventeen, before he had had any regular tutoring whatever. He later painted a second self-portrait – much more mature in style because of his subsequent training and experience, but reflecting nonetheless his early agility. This second portrait attracted some attention at the time, and has now joined the Peter Scheiwe collection in Münster, West Germany.

Beginning to be impressed by his son's painting, William Howley asked an art teacher named Frederick Sandys to examine it; and on the latter's advice Edward joined the Slade School in London in 1893. This was an important phase in his life. Not only did his fellow students include such artists as Eves, McEvoy, Campbell-Taylor, Bennett, and a host of others, many of whom became members of the Royal Academy or gold medalists in later years, but he was in distinguished company already. For among his tutors could be counted Tonks, Brown, Steer and Sargent. Each had their different methods of training. Henry Tonks, for example, 'a herring-gutted figure with a high bridge on his nose', as George Moore described him, would look long and ponderously at Edward's drawing on the artist's donkey – a four-legged stool with a rest for a drawing-board – and then say, 'Well, you know what's the matter with that,' and pass on; while the more patient and experienced John Sargent would firmly and unerringly pencil in the correct line.[2]

It was a happy, youthful time for Edward, and the students had their jokes. Reginald Eves in particular was teased by his colleagues, who later dubbed his enticing pictures of young ladies, 'Eves's flicks'! On one occasion during a life class when a nude female model swooned and all the students rushed to her assistance, the gallant Arthur McEvoy became so embarrassed at finding such a lady in his arms that he promptly lost courage and dropped her!

By 1894, after two years' attendance, Edward felt he had learned all he could at the Slade, and sought admission to the St John's Wood Art School. During this time, while living at 140 High Street near by, he gained admission to the Royal Academy School of Modelling from the Life, joining it early in 1896. What is believed to be his entry painting was no mean effort – a young girl in peasant costume, somewhat in the style of a Puritan maiden, which is now in the Scheiwe collection mentioned above. He worked on other figures for Academy School classes and competitions, among them his large oil, *Cleopatra before Caesar*. Later on he received a most pleasant surprise. In 1896 he won the coveted Creswick Award for the best landscape of the year. Its title was *A Farm on the Hill*, depicted in a Dorset setting, but the only known relic of its existence is one faded photograph. It intrigued Edward later to discover what had happened to it; artists are notoriously slack about keeping records. Letters survive from a Miss E. Brown of Cirencester and an E. Homan of Finchley enquiring after it, while evidence indicates that it was later purchased by a Mr Moreton, MP.[3] At all events his entry into the Royal Academy Antique School was assured over the next five years.

The Creswick Award carried a cash prize of £30 – modest in sound but significant in substance when measured against the purchasing power of money at the time (£100 in 1900 can be equated to about £4,000 in 1990). It is not known how Edward spent the money, except that he might have laid some aside for a coming trip to Italy, and it certainly proved useful for his immediate tutorial needs.

The following year, 1897, also brought good news. It must have been exciting for him to learn of his first success at Royal Academy exhibitions with the acceptance of his *A Farm on the Hill*. Other works were submitted to various exhibitions, among them his scenes of Sandsfoot. One of these depicts a castle by this name near Weymouth – romantic and poetic in texture, an ironclad in the distance, suggesting the drama of history in a way Turner might have wanted to express it. Completed by 1899, it was admired by all, including his family, though whether this particular view was submitted to the Royal Academy for this season remains unclear.[4]

Edward's intensive studies at the Academy School, reinforced by frequent student-pass visits to the National Gallery and other institutions, were relieved at the end of the century by a fruitful trip to Italy. Here he was accompanied by his friend Frank Bennett, a colleague at the Slade and winner of the coveted Gold Medal. Since this award consisted of £100, plus £30 for travel expenses, it must be assumed that Edward's father gave his son at least some supportive help to match.

Italy is a dream for any artist; and in coming down from Lucerne in Switzerland past the 7,000 ft. peak of Pilatus, past the carnivals in the little villages, Edward and Frank darted from one side of the railway carriage to the other to get breathtaking glimpses of the Lepontine Alps before entering the St Gotthard Tunnel, which leads to Lugano near the Italian frontier. They were heading for Florence.

'A fairy place . . .', Edward enthused in a letter to Frank's father in March 1900:

I have come to the conclusion that if these places are to be described, one must have some more degrees of comparison, one exhausts all one's superlatives! I shall never forget the delight of arriving at Florence in the quiet fresh light of a lovely dawn after a night in a fuggy railway carriage. I could hardly believe we had reached the goal at last, altho' I could not have had a more fitting morning for my first sight of a place that had been but a dream to me before, & it is little more now. Even after having seen its real beauties in my first sight of the Duomo & Giotto's Companile particularly, I was for some reason rather disappointed, perhaps because I could not realize it; I felt it was very beautiful & yet could not grasp it, but I can now that I have seen it often. I think when you first see a beautiful thing that is quite a strange sort of beauty to you, you are not, one cannot be, sufficiently in sympathy with it; to appreciate it requires digesting. The Cathedral, the Campanile, looks best at night, I think in a full light. . . . It is lovely too with the evening sun on it. It is curious how little you are impressed by its size on entering, I suppose on account of the enormous size of all the detail; one realizes it more when looking down on it from the dome; the great height gives you a funny feeling down the back! We have been doing the churches, such as are free! Not having obtained a *permesso* as artists for the galleries . . . we are in fear & trembling lest our letter [for an application] should have miscarried. . . . Santa Croce is glorious, full of lovely things, the Giotto frescoes so simple & earnest & such lovely colours, & then one bestrolls on one floor worn by many feet until but a suggestion remains of what was – a few lines like a sketch. Santa Maria Novella, San Michele, all so beautiful, but you know them. I wish some of our English churches took after them in decorating with works of Art; but I have seen nothing to beat Westminster, I think, as a building exterior or interior. Today we have been into the Uffizi and the Pitti [palaces] & enjoyed seeing the pictures immensely. A glorious Filippo Lippi which I only knew from reproduction, which gives no idea of its beauty & refined colour. We were very disappointed in the St John of Andrea del Sarto . . . the colour was very disagreeable. . . . We pray for better weather. . . . We tried to do some sketching last night but got very cold. Well I think I have occupied enough of your time. . . .

Yrs. very sincerely,
E.F. Wells

PS You will be glad to hear that the centimes & francs have dropped into their proper places in my mind![5]

In addition to Florence and Sienna, Edward visited Brescia in the north, and from there travelled to Ravenna, Viterbo, and Rome, including Tivoli. Thereafter in 1901 it was Naples, the isle of Capri, Sorrento, and Amalfi in the south. 'Arrived here yesterday from Capri,' he wrote to his mother in February from a hotel in Sorrento, 'Feel very homesick for Capri, had grown to love it . . .'.[6] Edward also saw Venice and the Dolomites, either before his trip south, or else on his way back to England.

These were surely among the happiest months of his life. Unattached at the age of twenty-four, he had a distinguished honour to his credit, good standing at the Royal Academy School, with enough to get by for a whole year's study in Italy. His prolific output during this Italian visit resulted in a fine collection of pen-and-ink drawings and sepia-wash and watercolour sketches, some of which are in the hands of various present-day collectors. The sensitive style of the tiny canvasses reveals a texture of multiform and lively colours – bright reds, deeper purples, poetic shades of green. There is something almost Grecian in the aura that envelops the marble, the bronze, the verdigris, against a backdrop of cypress walks and hills, blue sky – something architectonic in the faded grandeur he imparts to temples and statues, courtyards and fountains, urns and tombs. He was a skilful limner, good with light and shade, good at suggesting the drama of a story. Edward had fully captured the Classical spirit. Indeed some critics regard these scenes, from Venice to the Dolomites, from Viterbo to Capri, as among the most prized of his works.

Back in England later in 1901, Edward soon left the Royal Academy Antique School and finally rented No. 11 Onslow Studios in Onslow Place, Chelsea. He seems to have alternated his time between Chelsea and Evershot, where he would be eagerly greeted by his family and their staff. Then, at the turn of the century, he experienced a most successful one-man show in Dorchester of his Dorset and Italian paintings, consisting of 230 exhibits.

Opened in the Henry Duke Company's large property saleroom on South Street by 1902, the exhibition was an instant success. In this he was helped by the patronage of Helen, Countess of Ilchester, and her daughter, Lady Muriel Fox-Strangeways, not to mention supportive attendance by members of the Digby, Scott, Lethbridge and Bankes families, to name but a few. Singled out for special praise were Edward's paintings of the Ilchester home at Melbury, of Weymouth and Cattistock, the Blackmoor Vale, Chepstow Castle over-looking the Wye and scenes of Scotland, especially Struan. Among the Italian scenes viewers noted the pearly delicacy of lagoon and canal in cities like Florence and Venice, the translucent Adriatic, the stippled palaces, the deep-blue sea around Capri, the daring tints of people's garments reflected in the rippling water's edge under an Italian deep-blue sky.

Portraits by Edward at the exhibition included that of Mrs Edward Duke and her two daughters, one of Miss Ethel Skardon, and a pastel of his sister Maud playing the violin which he had completed three or four years before. Tragically, Maud's portrait, encased in a glazed frame, was subsequently wiped clean with a sponge by an over-zealous furniture remover in the 1960s when the glass had worked loose, and the pastel was wiped clean with it, leaving the picture a total ruin. Such is often the fate of precious works of art. (An oil work survives of Edward's sister, however, as well as a delightful

Interior by Candlelight in which Maud plays the violin accompanied by probably her mother at the piano.)

The Dorchester exhibition reflected one salient feature of Edward's work, namely, his growing versatility. Apart from draughtmanship with plain pencil and pastel he was equally at home with oil or watercolour, in portraiture or landscape, while his scenes of rural and family life, his still lifes and his later flower pieces, testify to his wide range of genre.

Back in London, ensconced in his modest studio in Onslow Place, Edward could weigh his prospects with a certain calm detachment. London offered a perfect chance for the development of his skill, undecided as he may have been as to which branch of it to pursue. He could also enjoy life. The big city at the turn of the century was then at the threshold of the Edwardian age (Queen Victoria had died in January 1901), and the young artist breathed in its Indian summer of Empire. Financially and imperially, London was the centre of the world. And it catered to every taste. There were the clubs of Piccadilly like the St James's, with the 'growler' cabs outside and the flower girls, where young swells in toppers and tails would chase down Bond Street in the early hours of the morning, 'hurling hot potatoes at the shops', to quote Edward's own words. There were promenaders in Hyde Park, the jammed oyster bars, the crowds jostling to board London's first electric trams. There were horse-buses carrying Union Jacks on their upper decks (ladies being chivalrously helped to mount the stairs thereto), and steam-driven trains on the Underground, or 'Drain', 'leaving a reek of sulphur in the mouth', again to quote Edward's own words. Then there were the theatres. Theatres galore, from the Alhambra to the Tivoli, with as many actors and actresses on stage. Among those whom Edward remembered were music-hall stars like Harry Lauder (his favourite comedian), Marie Lloyd, Lottie Collins, Ella Shields, George Robey, and a host of others. Their songs would echo via barrel organs down London streets. While superficially austere, perhaps, Edward was very human at heart, loving the common features of everyday life; but in order to earn his living, his time was necessarily taken up with the leisured sitters he was commissioned to paint. And there were times when formality and etiquette indeed held sway.

His joining the Chelsea Arts Club in February 1902 helped him to forge many contacts, though Helen, Countess of Ilchester, probably gave him his first commission locally. Many of his portraits at this stage were in pastel, as distinct from oil, and apart from Lady Helen's, such portraits included that of her daughter Lady Muriel, Lady Helen Stavordale (her daughter-in-law), the smiling and lively Veronica Fullbrook-Leggatt, Mrs J. Milne and son, two sisters of the Pellew family (Margaret and Caroline), besides that of his own sister Maud. These portraits were shown at the Carlton Gallery in 1904.

Edward had great success with pastels at this gallery. From April onwards periodicals like the *Queen* were praising the artist ('a coming man, for not only has he the good fortune to enjoy the highest patronage, but he evinces a powerful individuality in his portraits') – comments echoed in the *Ladies' Field*, the *Gentlewoman* and *Vanity Fair*. Later in 1904 a critic wrote in the *Queen*:

> A very important exhibition of pictures by Old Masters is now open at the [Carlton] Galleries as from 3 June. The pictures which are for sale have been drawn from important private collections, and should prove of very great interest to connoisseurs and collectors. Owing to the great interest created by Mr E.F. Wells's pastel portraits, Messrs Claude and Trevelyan Turner have arranged to keep a few of the most representative portraits on exhibition during the remainder of the season. . . .[7]

The Turner brothers were directors of the Carlton Gallery, and their support gave Edward an important boost. Indeed there seems to have been a close rapport between these promoters and the artist dating from the early years of the century. Nos. 5 and 15 of *Gowan's Art Books*, illustrating Reynolds and Raeburn respectively, for example, carried an announcement on the front page in which Claude and Trevelyan of the Carlton Gallery at Pall Mall Place as 'Purchasers and Sellers of Fine Pictures by the Best Old Masters invite the attention of anyone desiring Portraits in Pastel to the works of Mr E.F. Wells, the clever painter of Portraits in Pastel'.[8] Indeed, it is evident that Edward's work in this field was popular enough to warrant continued showings at the Carlton over the next four years. (Reference is also made to, among others, the miniaturist Edward Tayler.)

Where watercolours were concerned, another gallery that claimed Edward's attention at this time was that of the Dudley Art Society. Located in the Egyptian Hall, Piccadilly, before this was demolished in 1904/5, when it was moved to the Alpine Club premises in Conduit Street, this prestigious gallery generally received a wide range of press response. Earning special mention were Edward's *Bubb Down, Moorland Stream*, and *Early Morning* (the latter praised by the *Court Journal* as 'one of the best things in the exhibition'). The *Bazaar Exchange and Mart* was particularly supportive of Edward's work at the Dudley. It praised the virility of his *Primose Wood* ('where the tussocks of blossoms are delightfully rendered among a leafless wood which imprisons the air of spring'), the harmony of his *Chantrey Hill, Sussex*, and his desolate *Column on the Skirts of Dartmoor*. When it considered one exhibition very feeble, its writer stoutly commented on Edward: 'We are glad to find his work still giving a little snap to the Dudley tameness. . . . His drawings are always so homogeneous and the touch so easy.' Singled out for special mention were such works as *A Showery June* and *Wet Mist Over Exmoor* – praise generally shared by other periodicals.[9]

The *Bazaar* also gave high marks to Edward's work shown elsewhere, such as at the Modern Gallery. Here, among what the writer considered largely second-rate exhibits, Edward's paintings were cited as virtually the best, particularly his pastel, *Tea in the Hayfield*, as well as *The Manor Farm* and *A*

Fallen Tree, struck by lightning

Country Churchyard. Praise for the first-named work was also given by the *Globe* and the *Illustrated London News* (it had already been commended in the *Morning Post* when shown at the Carlton two years before); while the *Ladies' Pictorial* commented succinctly that,'with his vigorous touch he gets the sentiment of the scene into his canvasses'.[10]

As his landscapes and portrait commissions gathered momentum in the early years of the century, Edward sought perfection in the same proportion. But in the heyday of Edwardian England, with its glorious, if gilded, opportunities for an ambitious young artist, he never craved the glitter of publicity, even as the term 'an E.F. Wells painting' began to circulate among serious art lovers. He was never much of a showman. Nor was he a 'lady's man' in the style of a Reginald Eves. Rather, he was a detached professional, loyal to the tenets which his sitters demanded – 'true-representational' portraiture – while secretly attached to his greatest love, the landscape of rural

England by which he had been nurtured. He never really wanted to stray for long outside these limits. The landscape's poetry was to be brought in line with colour, the unceasing song fused into the image. He remembered Italy. And the price he paid was patience, observation, and a great deal of hard work.

On rare occasions he could work extremely fast with a portrait. His lovable nurse Clara Dennis, for example, he painted in five hours. Relaxed and in familiar surroundings, Edward surely found his greatest repose here at home. Indeed, he loved his frequent returns to Evershot, the talks with his parents, his trips among the fields and hills of Dorset. Nor was the sea too far away, accessible by train or bicycle. Here he would sometimes touch off an oil sketch in addition to watercolours – *The Golden Cap* near Charmouth is an example. At other times he could be as painstaking as if he were doing a professional job, inspired as he was where 'Thomas Hardy country' was concerned. For Edward was as attached to the soil as this writer was. One has only to consider his magnificent oil works and watercolours to recognize the deepest well-spring of his creative impulse – the oneness of man with nature.

Edward, a man of Dorset, his true spiritual home, was an active person, athletic and fast in his movements. Of average build, reserved, of neat, good-looking appearance (despite ears 'impishly pointed like an elf's', as someone put it), he would scour the landscape, probing with eye and brush, his own poise like part of nature itself. His paint-box and sketch-book were ever parts of his accoutrement. He worked with care always, whether working fast or slow. The tints of cloud, nuances of shade, the sweep of trees bent by the wind, were a challenge to him because they affected his soul. Not caring what the world might think, in the end he was exultant, sometimes exhausted, his greenish-hazel eyes intense beneath his 'dark shining hair'.

In the final analysis Edward was a loner – a devotee to traditional realism as he conceived it.

CHAPTER TWO

THE BATTLE OF STYLES

After an inner struggle as to what direction to pursue, Edward was making remarkable progress by the early years of the twentieth century. His work appeared no less than seven times in the Royal Academy from 1897 to 1912, almost an average of one acceptance every two years. Such success, however, was largely subordinate in his mind to his search for technical perfection, at which he worked with painstaking care.

But what technique was it? In this respect one should mention his training at the Royal Academy Antique School, to which he was admitted for a term of three years as from February 1896, and for a further term of two years as from January 1899. Here he received a thorough grounding in the basic principles of art as it was then taught. There was also his Italian venture. During this time evidence suggests he was interested, among other techniques, in those of the Pre-Raphaelite Brotherhood, though it was pure coincidence that a studio which he had occupied by 1908 was named after its leader, Rossetti. He was also devoted to Rembrandt, whom he regarded as arguably the greatest painter of all time. Turner was another idol. But Edward's main model as a source of study and illumination was undoubtedly Titian, the great Venetian colourist and copier from nature.

Endorsing this view are some notes in Edward's own hand taken from Charles Fresnoy's *De Arte Graphica* ('Treatise on Art'):

Titian copied Nature more correctly than anyone else. Zanetti wrote of his chiaroscuro that he used a light preparation of chalk or chalky primary, on which the colours laid on again & again produced the effect of a transparent veil surrounding the tints no less mellow than lucid. Strong shadows carried a finish with colour when dry to give their picture force & giving them more warmth when the sun is just merging into the middle tint.

Observations by Mengs on Titian: he was the first after the revival of painting to avail himself of the ideal in the different colours of dress. Before his time all colours were used indiscriminately & were laid on with the same

The artist as a young man, *c.* 1898

gradations of light & shade. Titian discovered that red serves to approximate objects, yellow to take in the rays of light, while azure is of use in
strong shadows. Nor was he less versed in colours of a more juicy nature.
Thus he could impart the same grace, clearness, & dignity of colouring to
his shades & middle tints as to his stronger lights, as well as diversify by a
final diversity of middle tints the different superficies of bodies. Nor did
anyone better know how to maintain the equilibrium of the three colours
[white, red & black], . . . difficult to be observed in practice.

Edward concluded his notes with a saying by Titian, handed down by
Boschini, that whoever would make himself a picture should make himself
thoroughly acquainted with the properties of white, red and black (as with a
bunch of grapes which Titian took as a simile for grouping his figures). In his
portraits he made the stronger lights fall on the eyes, nose and mouth, leaving
the other parts to indistinctness.[1]

Edward can indeed be described as a Titianist *par excellence*. But other
influences were at work. More tangibly, he got to know an old army captain
turned artist named Charles Henry Augustus Lutyens (1829–1915). Among
this man's many children, incidentally, were two artist sons, Frederick and
Ned, the latter better known as Sir Edwin Landseer Lutyens who became
President of the Royal Academy.

Charles Lutyens (and to some extent his older son Frederick) made an
impact on Edward. Even more so did Edward's own father, William Howley
Wells. Indeed these two senior men, Charles Lutyens and Howley Wells,
traditionalist as they were in critical attitudes, were familiar with each other's
views and pursued parallel aims. As for Edward, it was possibly through his
father's prompting that he got to know Charles Lutyens in the first place, and
the latter's address at 16 Onslow Square, being near to Edward's studio at
Onslow Place after 1901, enabled them to keep in close contact.

Son of a British general of Dutch-German origins, Charles Lutyens saw
service in Montreal, Canada, and in the Crimea, and sketches by him were
made in both these places. Indeed from 1862 to 1903 Lutyens' work was
exhibited regularly at the Royal Academy. Horse-portraiture became one of
his specialties, and the story goes that being a keen rider, Lutyens on one
occasion suddenly stopped instructing his soldiers in musketry while they
were on parade, then jumped on his horse to join the chase of a local hunt that
was passing by! But Lutyens had other passions; and one of these was his
claim to have rediscovered the so-called Venetian secret in which he tried
unsuccessfully to interest the Royal Academy.

Variously described, this was said to be an ancient formula for obtaining a
luminous shade of red used by the great Venetian masters, including Titian.
Another version gives it as a measurement of the effects of nature which can
be as accurate as sound, while yet another describes it as a system of tonal
perspective obtained by underpaintings.[2] What is significant is that no one

was versed at the time in probing the mystery of this technique – except for a very few, who included Charles Lutyens and William Howley Wells. It is of interest that both men designed instruments for measuring tone and colour by reflection, Charles having also designed a contraption for judging distances for long-range artillery. Both men also became interested in light phenomena, and from here it was but a short step in the search for accurate true-to-nature tonal reproduction on canvas. It is not known for certain how either man got interested in the technique or who 'rediscovered' the secret first. The important point is that both of them took the quest seriously enough to devote a large part of their lifetimes unearthing its relevance to art in an age of shifting values at the turn of the century.

Stern critic of what he considered slapdash methods of art instruction, and whose own services in the art schools were on this account rejected, Lutyens studied ways of preserving the luminous flesh tones in painting from nature pursued by masters such as Titian. Many besides Titian incidentally, from Giorgione to Dutch and Spanish masters, including Rembrandt and Veláz-quez, had pondered this same problem. Decrying the blatantly crude colouring in vogue at the time because in his view it reflected garish shoddiness instead of the fundamentals of a serious, solid movement, the old man would claim as his support the outcries of both press and public, in which even the artists themselves would complain of one picture killing another. 'What with this Royal Academy . . . they know nothing about pictures,' Lutyens wrote to Edward, 'It is for a future people to know this. The way things are going is cruel beyond belief. . . . Bad pictures produced everywhere and the vastest sums given for almost rubbish.'[3]

Edward was impressed by this concern for good standards in art, by this sympathy for the artist's plight. 'Where indeed are we going, to whom do we turn?' he might have asked himself cautiously. Both Lutyens and his own father were there to respond to his uncertainties. 'A young artist striving after tone in his pictures,' wrote William Howley Wells in his notes of 1905–8, 'might well, after studying all the various ideas of colour tone represented on the walls of an exhibition of modern pictures, exclaim in the words of Pilate, "What is truth?", as applied to true tone in painting.'[4]

One encouraging event in an attempt to rival the Academy, incidentally, had been the founding in 1877 of the Grosvenor Gallery in Bond Street by Sir Coutts and Lady Lindsay (Blanche Rothschild). Richly furnished and spacious, this gallery was designed to allow for pictures to be hung widely apart, often in groups by the same hand, such as that of Burne-Jones or of Whistler; and Edward himself exhibited here in later years.

At this point it is pertinent to consider the competing trends in art at the turn of the century in terms of style, design, and taste. Three general groups can roughly be discerned. Firstly, there were the conservative traditionalists already mentioned, though William Howley Wells of course, while an excellent designer and experimenter with light and optics, was not a practising artist.

Then we have Edward himself, Charles Lutyens and his son Frederick, along with artists like Frank Bennett and Vivian Rolt, among others. John Hanson Walker could also be roughly classed among these, at least in his results; and Edward himself spoke of a Moynihan whom he would also include, though whether he was referring to the more recent P. Moynihan is unclear. For want of a better term this group can be labelled 'Titianists' or 'True Tonalists' – they generally experimented with luminosity as a vital factor of 'true tone' in painting.

Secondly, there were those who accepted the shifting standards of the Royal Academy and benefitted from associating with it. Upholding the general concept of order, harmony, and unity, many were RAs who had earned their status not only through merit but also through accepting the views of the Establishment, whose higher echelons of professional society they had breached. In short, they accepted the status quo. Distinguished artists of this type included Richmond and Poynter ('What can you expect when the leading painters are Sir W. Richmond and Sir E. Poynter? A tyranny, that's what it is,' fumed Charles Lutyens in a letter to Edward).[5] Among other artists in this category were Frederick Leighton, George F. Watts, Alfred Waterhouse, Arthur Stockdale Cope, W.H.Y. Titcomb, and Gerald Kelley. The list is legion, though some of them overlapped, or had connections, with other groups.

Lastly, at the opposite end from the conservative traditionalists were those who were influenced in varying degrees by Impressionism (and later, Post-Impressionism). This was a powerful group that, defying Royal Academy traditions and much public opinion in England, banded together to form the New English Art Club. Impressionism, originating in France with Manet and others, and further back, in Spain with Goya, reached England in the eighties of the last century. Its technique might be roughly defined as the transposition of colour values to another key in order to simulate the general effect of light. Members of the New English Art Club did not openly call themselves Impressionists as a general rule, but were interested in the technique and reflected this in many of their works. Artists joining it included James McNeill Whistler, Walter Richard Sickert, Henry Tonks, James Guthrie, John Lavery, James Shannon, P. Wilson Steer, Fred Brown, M. Lindner, Edward Stoll, Stanhope Forbes, Frank Bromley, and Maurice Greiffenhagen. Others associated with the Club or showing Impressionism's influence were such artists as Brake Baldwin, James Pryde, Margaret Macdonald, Everett Shinn, Gwen John, William Orpen, Jacques-Emile Blanche, and Augustus John. Critical of the Club, incidentally, for its allegedly feeble stand against the Academy Establishment, for its repetitious subjects and lukewarm Impressionism was the great exponent of the latter – W.R. Sickert, who in 1911 founded the Camden Town Group. Joining it were Spencer Gore, Harold Gilman and Robert Bevan, among others, including Camille Pissarro's son, Lucien.

The hostility of many segments of the British public was directed toward these latter groups not because they flirted with Impressionism as such, but because it was French (or so it was regarded, even though English painters like Turner had arguably played a role in its inception). There was a touch of pure xenophobia here. When an exhibition of French Impressionists' work was given in London in 1905, for example, it was coolly received. Old Academicians would look down their noses at the avant-garde oddities on the grounds that they might corrupt the young. As Paul Durand-Ruel, the French dealer who organized the exhibition, put it: 'The ironic consequence of this insular resistance to modern French painting is that Impressionism was old-fashioned before it was fashionable in England.'[6]

Those supporting the 'grey zone' between the two extremes, on the other hand, that is, the friends of the Establishment at the Academy, spent money freely on what were often third-rate British pictures, many of them totally worthless today. As standards fell in the Edwardian era, Charles Lutyens and William Howley Wells saw more and more justification for their arguments. 'The very cruellest institution in the world,' wrote Lutyens to Edward in familiar vein, referring to the Royal Academy, 'I heard Millais say when V. Princep [Valentine Prinsep] married a rich woman, "Think it well. He will now be able to give dinners."'[7] Lutyens, like Millais, knew what wining and dining meant – the constant social climb toward RA status, whether for oneself on the way up, or for others when you're at the top. (Shades of other institutions as well!) And Howley Wells said as much when he called the Academy judges 'hopeless people'. He doubted whether it was worth while for his son to enter any further paintings until he had made his name outside and could force them to accept him, as others had done. Somewhat prophetically where the Camden Town Group was concerned and no doubt reflecting the Grosvenor, Howley Wells proposed that rejected artists ought to set up a rival gallery of their own.[8]

With the lines of debate drawn and the acrimony sharpened, Lutyens so fulminated against every aspect of the Academy, including its long line of contributors, that anyone reading his letters to Edward might think he had an obsession against the Academy itself:

> They could make lots of good pictures instead of lots of bad ones, and it would not be so beastly cruel as it is now – and all this silly objection for the sake of a little variety. . . . I think I have at least directed you on the right course: to know the arts are in a terrible state. I have tried to put it right, but no thanks – scorn and hatred. . . . I hope you will have good luck at the RA. . . . I have been right in practitioning against the modern style of painting – which is all ignorance, unkindness, and jobbery.[9]

Nor did dealers escape his ire: 'I hear you think you have found the great [Venetian] secret. I hope indeed you have, for it would be a capital way out of the great difficulties we are in . . . and it will puzzle the dealers most extremely. They will wonder where they are. There have been great injustices done.'[10] He heaped scorn on Academicians and jobbers alike. But perhaps his unkindest cut of all was his slighting of individual painters both past and present, along with the inflated prices many Old Masters were getting. A Gainsborough for example, fetched £40,000 in 1911 'for a very faulty composition'. And Lutyens's contemporary, Holroyd, came in for particular criticism: 'What does Sir J. Holroyd know what is important! I should like to sweep all his humbug away, but as I said, people don't care a dump except for their own names and comforts.' Even the great Whistler was castigated: 'I was not listened to years ago. How different things might be – no silly hundred thousand pictures, no silly Whistler and his friend. . . . Oh the foolishness of the whole thing – the rot Claude Philipps writes – the misguiding nonsense. I should like much to give him a good dig in the ribs. Stupid ass. How he will hate me if things come right.'[11]

Edward's triumphant *Shower of Gold*, when it was exhibited at the Royal Academy in 1911 (discussed in the next chapter), cooled Lutyens's ire somewhat – after all, Edward was on his side. But not much. As if to give full vent to his feelings, he wrote:

> I saw your picture but could not see any pictures properly on account of my eyes – but what I did see made me say, "Oh!". It looked somehow as if they had all gone mad. The men who have done this are Ruskin, Leighton, Millais, Burne-Jones, Rossetti & others. What a pity . . . At the RA I did see one picture properly . . . Lavery's *White Horse*. What a shame to let such a thing in. Of course he will get worse & worse. Horse painting! What a horse. And Poynter's oak staircase. How sad, how very sad. Never mind – Hope, Hope, that is all one can do.[12]

Lutyens's scorn softened a little when he got on to a favourite topic – playing with 'bleographs' [biographs?], which included a primitive device for turning crude colours into true-tone images – 'capital pictures', he would enthuse. But soon the invective would return. It was a game with him. The old man was bitter, very bitter – and bigoted. But, surprisingly, Edward did not resent Lutyens' disgruntlement, perhaps because the latter struck in him a chord of sympathy on account of his honest search for truth. Lutyens also taught him a great deal. In no way a bigot himself, Edward probably reasoned that a little whiplashing of the Academy never did anyone any harm – social climbers least of all.

As for William Howley Wells, he was just as forthright and outpouring in argument, except that, unlike Lutyens, his shaft was not cast at individuals so much as on behalf of a principle: the principle of true tone in painting. He worked at this very hard. The details are complicated – he himself admitted they were difficult to explain in writing – and are well served by first quoting his words in connection with the formation of the New English Art Club, mentioned above:

Presuming that the merits of the Impressionism School consist in its aim at getting a true effect of light such as nature gives . . . and that its demerits in the eyes of its opponents were its inability to combine with its true effect of light a more general detail of the subjects treated, it follows that a method which would combine both a true effect of light without subordinating general detail so much, should be welcomed by both sides of the question. There is not the slightest reason that general detail should be subordinated in any way & at the same time that a true effect of light should be given. The combination is obtained by following nature's colours, absolutely truly, by a transposition of its values to a lower key in their true colours. The difficulty is to find a means of transposing nature's values to a lower key, in which every variety of object & hue under every lighting can be truly represented in nature's colour. Having once found this means, the combination mentioned above that Velázquez & other great masters of that school seem to have mastered, is possible.[13]

On this and other themes, Howley Wells (in between his bouts of shooting with Lord Ilchester in Dorset and Wiltshire) engaged in frequent correspondence with his son. It is only a pity that, while his letters to Edward in this context have survived, Edward's letters to his father have not.

As early as 1902, when Edward had left St John's Wood to live in Onslow Place, Howley Wells was writing to his son about his 'true-tone' experiments. Aware of the quest by Charles Lutyens and his son Frederick toward the same end, he cautioned Edward on many occasions not to reveal his findings to anyone (Frank Bennett included), even to the extent of destroying his information if necessary as he had drafted copies of his own. He admitted later, however, that artists would find it out anyway, give no credit to the originator, and 'simply crib it in their own way.'[14] He was referring loosely to what he termed the 'Venetian secret', in the same way that Lutyens did.

As implied above, this concerned the technique adopted by the Old Masters in seeking true tone in painting. Generally it involved the use of terms in a way any investigator wanted them to mean. In Howley Wells's specific case it meant a search to accurately grade and match colours in their correct tones from light to dark, and to establish correctly a tone scale for each colour and hue. The study of luminosity would play a big role in this. At the heart of his ideas was what he described as the 'middle tint', which was partly a measurement by the eye of the sky's reflected light. To put it in his own words:

The sky's reflections are in half tone to earth's reflections and invariable in their difference because as one is lighted up so is the other in proportion. There is not a shadow of a doubt in my mind that this is the whole Venetian secret, except the law of angles necessary to be applied in order to get the various degrees of shades, as an object is turned to or from double lightings. In studio work this direct light from the high side-light window takes the place of the sun & this reflected light of the sky is that from the ceiling or upper, subdued sky-lighting. One can understand why Sir Joshua & others chose a side-lighting more or less . . . .[15]

The next month, in March 1902, Howley Wells made a 'great' discovery – that, among other things, the middle tint reflected from the sky is half the middle tint reflected from the earth:

> Eureka!! Eureka!! [he wrote ecstatically to Edward] It is all plain now. The mystery of the middle tint is heaven's own mystery. Everything is, under sunlight, lighted up & shaded as follows: an object in full light is lighted by the direct sunlight and the reflected light from the sky according to the angle that the object is turned to or from direct from sunlight or sky. The range between the highest & lowest tone of the portion of the object in light being sunlight and middle tint reflected from the sky. An object in shadow is lighted by the reflected light from the sky and the reflected light from earth . . . the range being middle tint reflected from the sky, and middle tint reflected from the earth. Middle tint reflected from the sky is *half* middle tint reflected from the earth. You have taken the middle tint of the earth in your grey tint on the tone drawing of the white box. The sky & middle tint is *half* that. It is a lovely theory . . . but head-achy as Lutyens's. . . .[16]

The 'white box' mentioned above refers to a development from a box-sextant, an instrument used for measuring the angular distance of objects by means of reflection. Howley Wells had gone up to Barrow at 4.30 a.m. one morning early in March 1902, as the sun was just topping the hill. As it lit up the side of his white box, he observed that the top of the box was apparently half way in tint between the lit end of the box and the side of the box, thus revealing the earth's middle tint, which he was trying to determine. From here he evolved a new theory for his son to utilize, namely, that the proportions in luminosity between the three sides of the box – one facing the sun, one facing the sky (the middle tint), and the far one reflecting the earth or vertical canvas – can provide a scale for matching colours in the same relation, thus providing a 'true-tone' key for painting the colours on canvas.[17] He later built a more complex instrument with adjustable tubes and reflectors to this effect.

Three years later, in 1905, Howley Wells drafted an outline of documents explaining his theory of 'true tone in painting'. This set out a method for obtaining a true scale of colour tones in the colour matching process which his white-box device facilitated.

In his outline he wrote that, in order to avoid the situation where different artists rendered the same landscape with different tones, a proper scale of nature's true-tone colours was required. The eye alone was not enough. A method of guidance for the eye was therefore to be sought, along with a test for matching true tones with the painting on the canvas, albeit in a slightly lower scale of illumination. But difficulties abounded, he admitted, in matching nature's true colour tones correspondingly in paint. Nature's tones were brighter than obtainable by paint on a vertical canvas, unless the fullest light were brought upon it. The very limitation of paint was another problem, not to mention the need to eliminate the encumbrance of the matching process itself in the ordinary course of painting.

In dealing with the above problems, Howley Wells then elaborated further on the principles of his 'white box'. One side needed to face the sun, the top side the sky, and the far vertical side away from the sun so as to be white in shade like the vertical canvas to be painted on (the painter's limit for representing white in sunshine in his picture). If the box were multi-coloured, Howley Wells continued, there would be the same limit for representing nature's various hues in sunshine on the canvas. Since every exterior object is lit from three sources – sunlight, skylight, and vertical or earth's reflected light – every hue to be painted in any of the three types of lighting has to be painted in its proper colour proportionate in tone to the corresponding light source, be it sunshine, skylight, or earth's reflected light, as the vertical side of the box in shade is to the side of the box in sunshine. The same rule applied to all sunshine effects. All nature's colours needed to be toned down in proportion

Cornfield in Sussex

as the vertical side of the box in shade was to the side of the box in sunshine.[18]

A further development of Howley Wells's box method in seeking true-tone painting was his adjustable tubed instrument containing reflectors, which he increasingly mentions in the same documents. Specifically, its purpose was to raise the illumination of the canvas away from earth's reflected light ('earth vertical') to skylight, or from skylight to full sunlight, depending on the effect desired on the canvas in the interest of true-tone painting. In relation to the far side of the box (that is, the side away from the sun, or the next more highly illuminated side), the tube at full length altered the illumination of the canvas from earth vertical to skylight, or from skylight to full sunlight. For fainter sunlight and half-light effects, the increase in brightness from skylight to sunlight on canvas was done by simply shortening the tube and reducing the darkness thereby.[19]

In Howley Wells's view such devices were necessary because many artists erred in the task of matching by eye. They resorted to false colours in order to get apparent tone, and having no rule of true colour to guide them, could not retrieve true tone. But as a result of his research Howley Wells claimed that he had devised the means to allow painters to follow nature's true colour tones perfectly and in their proper relation, whatever the illumination in nature might be. With nature as true teacher, such a method would apply to all conditions of painting nature's colour tones in the true key and in the correct proportionate scale, whether out of doors or in the studio.

Howley Wells invited criticism of his ideas. The question was whether tone in art was to be subjective and varied, or determined by nature's true colour tones, remembering that colour and tone could not be separated from each other. But he did not want to stifle individual initiative; quite the reverse. Bearing in mind the proverb, 'Art is long, life is short,' he claimed that the artist would achieve more by adhering to a perfected rule of tone than any 'rule of thumb'. Following nature's scale of colour brought not only a harmony of colours but a true colour perspective, in which every object took its proper position and stood out from others as in nature. This was the antithesis to flatness in art. But where do we find any definite rule nowadays, Howley Wells complained, beyond a black-and-white tone, and sometimes not even this.[20]

Howley Wells's remaining documents from 1906 to 1909 largely concern experiments with his later tone-matching instrument mentioned above, consisting of adjustable tubes and reflectors. This applied specifically to his researches into optics, colours and hues, in which he frequently exchanged ideas with his son.[21]

In turning his attention to luminosity as a factor in true-tone painting, Howley Wells studied the work of such eminent spectral scientists as Sir John Herschel and Sir William Abney, both of whom made significant advances in physical optics, colour vision, and telescopy.[22] Abney also engaged in experiments with red and infra-red light.

But Howley Wells contributed ideas of his own above and beyond what spectral analysts generally had advanced; and some idea of his trend of thought concerning the use of his tubed instrument can be seen in the intricate conclusions he derived from his research in the latter part of his documents on true tone. Here emphasis is given to matching colours in their true tone, to fixing them to a scale of illumination by means of his instrument, and to adjusting them in their different lightings, whether sunlight, skylight, or earth's reflected light on the vertical plane (i.e. painting at right angles to full light) for transfer on to canvas. Such a method allowed for painting both out of doors and in the studio.[23] Emphasis is also given as part of this process to lustre in colour, leading to the action of white on black to the point of extinction, following Abney's rules, but space does not permit a detailed examination of this aspect. He also wrote about hue as an important factor in lustre and luminosity. As light was raised or lowered on colours, he explained, hue was taken out, in which process his instrument could be used to transfer natural hues to canvas accordingly.[24]

He ended his documents with some concluding remarks dated 25 July 1908. All colours rose and fell, he pointed out, equally from one illumination to another, but the same illumination acted differently on and between the individual colours, according to their colour from white to black. Hence, to find the colours due to the illumination in the original lighting, all colours needed to be brought to their base illumination according to the light of the day. This base was obtained by raising the illumination of the canvas to the full illumination of the light on the colour – sunlight or skylight as the case may be, according to whether the colour was in light or shade.[25]

Excerpts from Howley Wells's later correspondence with Edward from 1906 to 1909, which paralleled the outline draft of his documents on true tone in painting, show the high degree of confidence which passed between them. It was a close father-to-son relationship. In many contexts Howley Wells hoped his research was proving useful for Edward's painting practice, and gladly agreed to pay his railway fare from London to avoid any delay in his gaining access to all this vital knowledge. But, on the father's part at least, there seems to have been a fine line drawn between dedication and obsession. As this applied to Charles Lutyens as well, Edward, it seems, was being encouraged to further his technique by two zealous enthusiasts, his father in particular remaining as curious as ever about the other's findings:

> Be careful in talking to Lutyens . . . My instrument seems to me a 'marvel' now & we must be careful of it. . . . You have something to look forward to when you come here. It is all complete and written out now in case any accident happened to me meanwhile, as it must not be lost to mankind. . . . I believe it to be a solution of the theory of painting never known unless possibly to the Old Masters, certainly not [thus far] to Lutyens, judging by his painting.[26]

But fear lest Lutyens might have 'got it right' continued to haunt Howley Wells.

His worrying about Lutyens was not directed at him personally, but simply because he was genuinely concerned that a colleague might steal a march on him and somehow ruin the thrust of his objectives. It was his son whose work he was fighting for, just as Lutyens was exhorting his favourite son Frederick. So concerned was Howley Wells with security that for portrait painting he even devised a means of concealing his instrument from public view! All experimenters, after all, are anxious to control their own experiments. But Howley Wells could be almost as censorious in regard to Edward himself if he felt he was slipping in standard: 'I think you will still do more perfect work . . . when you have the latest practical development of my theory to work on,' he urged. In other contexts he complained that Edward's pictures here and there were not perfect in colour, or too low in tone. 'I can quite understand Lutyens not thinking that I have got the whole thing yet, as of course your late pictures are not even yet painted on the perfected method, and Anne Pellew's full-length is certainly not right. He will probably change his mind when he sees the next lot of pictures.'[27]

But as time went on he became more aware of his son's advancing technique, and so his instruction and criticism softened. A few excerpts from his letters of 1908 illustrate the point:

Nothing seems necessary but the tones of certain test colours to be made as I said, and which I require your help in before we can use the system perfectly. I think our minds from what you say in your last letter have been working on the same line of theory, viz., that all colours must be matched in full light to start with, be reduced to their common or true colour and be reproduced in their true black-and-white tones according to their similarities, every shade or hue of colour having its own especial luminosity.[28]

. . . I agree with you that I do not think we shall quite reach all colours in sunshine near white in half-light, but the beauty of the new find [a means to transfer colour shade to canvas corresponding to its black-and-white tone] is that it tells me exactly where one is in reaching illumination & if certain colours are beyond half-light. . . .[29]

. . . I think there is no doubt you are right in thinking that there are equal gradations of luminosity from the top light downward on all colours similarly, which is that the tube raises equally all colours from lighting to lighting equally, as nature does in the shaded tones, but it is essential first to get the top colours in their proper lighting according to their respective luminosities in order that these equal shade tones may start from a true basis of colour, otherwise they become too low in tone & lose purity. . . .[30]

That Howley Wells was a meticulous observer of colour phenomena is obvious from his many letters and documents. His experience as an engineer well equipped him to delve into the sciences of optics and luminosity, along with the gadgets that were his forte. He invented an adjunct to an easel, for example, by which colour was transferred to canvas corresponding to its black-and-white tone with no reflector being necessary, as well as a palette attachment for use in the colour-matching process.[31] He also intended to patent his long and short tube tone-matching instrument. Shortly before his death in 1909, a letter revealed his interest in purchasing polarizing photo-meters used in connection with spectroscopes (for comparing the intensity of one particular colour constituent in two different sources of light). The letter referred to a German supplier named Schmidt and Haensch, of Berlin.[32] It would be interesting to match Howley Wells's ideas with the principles of modern colour photography, then in its infancy.

By and large Edward was lucky to have the father he did. Strongly influential as he was, there is no evidence that he domineered or sought to impose upon his son a rigid style of painting hostile to other 'schools'. Rather, he was genuinely supportive of Edward's struggle to improve his technique – with realism admittedly, but in a spirit of moderation toward other traditions, Impressionism included. Aware that his son had taken up a rather hazardous profession, with no firm guarantee of income, he also strove doggedly to secure commissions for him, that from the Trafford family being a case in point.

As for Edward, his letters to his father, as noted already, have unfor-tunately been lost (perhaps his father destroyed them for reasons of security); but there is no doubt he responded to his father's many ideas and exper-iments. He learnt all about the 'middle tint' theory, how to use the true-tone tubed reflector instrument in the matching process, both for sunshine and skyscape, how to measure half-light and understand it, how to separate colour from hue with his knowledge of luminosity and lustre, and how to impart patina to the canvas. And while there is no evidence that Edward always used his father's instruments, he was manifestly influenced by their principles. Even without this support, however, Edward would probably have continued in the same 'true-representational' direction. Both eschewed what they considered sloppy standards in art. For them, as with others, it was the flagship of realism to which they clung.

Despite other critics, besides his father and the Lutyens pair, prepared to wage the battle, as the century progressed Edward became aware of the ever-widening gap between his own pure brand of 'Titianism' and the public's brand of seemingly declining taste. His work being neither main-stream nor decadent, in the course of time its isolation became even more apparent. While not despising societies like the New English Art Club or the Camden Town Group, and, indeed, conceding the importance of movements such as Impressionism, or even Cubism later, as respectable paths for those who wanted to pursue them, he himself chose not to. Lone craftsmanship, not following a trend, was his instinctive practice. Perhaps his friend and fellow artist, Vivian Rolt, put it best, writing in 1922: 'Pleased to see you stick to solid traditions. It will come back I hope; anyway our Training does not seem to fit us for the ultra modern School.'[33]

Ironically, Edward's panel portrait of Vivian Rolt conveys a strikingly unfinished, 'modern', effect, as if unwittingly disproving Rolt's own statement. And the same experimentation applies to the symbolism in a sketch he made of himself as a sun god around 1928 in the heyday of the Chelsea Art Ball. One feels that he could have mastered any style he wanted to. True-tonal realism, however, remained his basic creed. And although it would seem that when Frederick Lutyens, with whom Edward entertained a friendship throughout, died in 1924, the 'Venetian secret' might have died with him, this was not so. For, thanks in part to the interest shown by Frederick's father, and especially to the persistence of his own father, it was passed on safely to Edward, who remained one of the very few who knew of it.[34]

CHAPTER THREE

EARLY MATURITY

By the late 1890s Edward was becoming closely acquainted with one Anne Helen Pellew, who was then approaching her twentieth year. Daughter of an Indian Civil Service judge who became Commissioner of Dacca (a friend of Edward's parents), and of Dorothy Mary Anderson, whose father was a clergyman, Anne was a fair product of Victorian England – loyal to her traditions, resourceful and accommodating. By 1910 they were married. Anne adored Edward, but she was also very delicate, and Edward proved his love, correspondingly, by ministering to her every need, consoling her with attentiveness and patience. In a word, the marriage was to prove a happy and durable one through much adversity.

Anne Pellew's forthright intelligence in handling practical matters where Edward's personal affairs were concerned was shown as early as November 1899 in a letter which she wrote to his mother from her home at Rodney House in Clifton:

> I am afraid Eddie must think me very remiss, not having sent his [damaged] tie back before, but I have been seeing if I could match it in vain before cutting the end off, which I had to do in the end as all the shops said they wouldn't be able to get any stuff in the least like it for me. I hope Eddie won't think it very patchy. . . . I have been organ'g a concert on Monday, quartets . . . & last night I went to dinner to Hugo [Pellew] to meet Dr Buck, the Cathedral organist & his wife, they are so nice & he is going to give me singing lessons. I hope you are all flourishing & Clara quite recovered. Tell her I was so disappointed I didn't see her at the show, we all looked out for her. . . .
>
> Ever your loving Anne H. Pellew[1]

Her letter to Edward written shortly afterwards reveals a natural growing confidence in their relationship, though many years were to pass before they would marry:

> . . . I don't quite know what you mean about 'shy', if it is that you find it bores you to write I'd much rather you didn't tho' otherwise I must confess

Anne Pellew or *Sibyl*, the artist's first wife, *c*. 1905

I am always delighted when I get a letter – from *anyone!* I've been doing quite a lot of things since I came home, it has been a regular whirl of excitement, at the same time I have managed to read a good deal, have bought six more penny poets & have been reading Shakespeare's *Sonnets*, Coleridge's *Christobel* & lots more. I do wish I could see Sandsfoot [Castle] with that & these pictures; to think that you will know next Saturday! Maud is going to stay for it isn't she? & I suppose you will both go home on the Monday after. What did you think of Sarasate, he is extraordinary but I rather wish he played more classical music; it is my ambition to hear Joaquin. . . .

Yours very sincerely,
Anne H. Pellew[2]

After his return from Italy, newly ensconced in his studio in Onslow Place, Edward concentrated on his painting even as thoughts of Anne were never far from his mind. And though professional expertise was forthcoming from his father, it was his mother he listened to more, perhaps, in a deeper emotional sense. 'Our artist has to put up with much,' she wrote, 'but never mind, your day is coming, *everything* comes to him who knows how to wait with courage; fate is always conquered by patience & determination.'[3]

With his mother's words ringing in his ears, Edward took consolation in seeing as much of Anne as convention would allow. Whenever she came up from Clifton she might be accompanied by any of her family, including her own six siblings. There were the usual house parties, gatherings at the maternal home in Wimbledon, the exhibitions and concerts, and of course visits to Evershot. One special haunt was Fulham Road, not too far from his studio, where they could be seen together in the then fashionable Bohemian restaurants.

It might seem surprising that Edward became interested at this stage in character reading – not as a whim, but in earnest, by professional 'seers'. Perhaps it was his way of controlling his impatience, of sublimating his desires. In 1904, as a young man not long out of art school, Edward was in no position to marry. So this kind of analysis, very much in vogue at the time brought its romantic compensations. Anne was a delicate flower. As such, Edward would seek every means, even prophetic graphology if necessary, to convince himself that fate would inflict no harm on the lady of his choice. Artist to the core, he was taking no chances with the stars.

That Anne passed the test (along with the seers themselves in terms of fairly accurate descriptions of their subject) is clear from the surviving reports of her analysis, written in the Fulham district from 1904 onwards. One such document reads in part:

The subject of this study is artistic, poetical, enthusiastic and of a highly-strung temperament. . . . Not only in affairs of the heart would she be . . .

intense, in Religion or Art she would show the same white heat of . . . enthusiasm and service; in fact this subject would make a religion of work or the development of any of the deep traits of character. . . . She is a lover of music and should be an accomplished pianist, but this character is many-sided, so that any particular work she takes in hand she would bring to a successful issue. Altogether this is a splendid type of a very highly developed gentlewoman.

W. Smith

Four days later Edward had himself analysed by the same man, who again gave a generally accurate picture of his subject (though Edward, contrary to the seer's report, was neither a good dancer nor of a capricious nature):

This gentleman is decidedly original in ideas and develops them on practical lines; he has imagination and a deep insight into the material and spiritual side of life. He is many-sided, and in Art . . . he is a Genius, has great tenacity of purpose and a dogged determination to succeed; he does nothing half-heartedly. This subject has a passion for work, and if he stops it is only to rest, returning with vigour, inspiration and enthusiasm. Has strong will power but at times willing to allow himself to float with the tide; on such occasions his subconscious self or brain is collecting new materials, as the subject cannot be idle. He makes a lasting impression upon all those with whom he comes in contact and is individual in all his work. He is a master in the grouping and arrangement of colours and nothing harsh in treatment can come from his brain, therefore his work is executed with a peculiar subtlety of feeling and delicacy of treatment and is finished with dignity and grandeur. He cannot show the deeper side of his nature where there is no affinity of ideas. He would make a very desirable companion in hours of leisure or on a holiday tour; on such occasions he would enter into the spirit of the moment with abandon. He loves the free, bracing life of the country but has a natural capacity to make himself at home under any conditions. He has many traits of 'Mark Tapley' in his character [a tavern type in Dickens's *Martin Chuzzlewit*, renowned for his indomitable good humour]. Toward ladies he is chivalrous and studies their moods. At the dance he makes an excellent partner. He has a capacity for singing and music and were he not so nervous would be a success in Opera or on the concert stage – there is ability shown in acting either in comedy or tragedy. He is capricious and a little exacting at times and is capable of being sarcastic, but his knowledge of human nature and his reluctance to hurt the feelings of anyone, dominates this trait and he would not bring it into play except in moments of anger when his higher emotions are some-times forgotten. At the present time his health is good, but occasionally he suffers from lassitude and nervous depression; it cannot be otherwise with a character possessing so much nervous energy. He has tact, and is diplomatic in a marked degree. The lower desires have had to make place for the higher and altruistic ego to a great extent, but he is a man of the world in a very true sense. This is a remarkable character and a dissector of human nature.

W. Smith[4]

Another 'seer' in the Fulham district for whom Edward had a special regard was one named 'Alastor', and their correspondence lasted many years. His report on Anne reads:

The subject of this study has great mental ability, the force of intelligence for outweighing physical strength becoming so pronounced that it is scarcely possible for her to rest, the brain planning and working out the creation of new ideas, colour schemes, subjects for the canvas etc. . . . She has the courage of her convictions but physical inability prevents her (at times) from carrying them into effect, thus causing restlessness; this, however, may be overcome, as rest of mind brings bodily vigour, and the Universal Heart desires to bring every throb and pulse of His creation into complete harmony. . . .

Alastor[5]

Perhaps Alastor's optimism about Anne's future and interest in poetry and the cosmic order explain Edward's trust in him; indeed, he was mentioned many times by Edward in later years. At all events Anne's delicate health never detracted Edward from his choice, nor did the large family of marriageable candidates she came from. As well as two brothers (Hugo and John Edward) Anne had four sisters – Dorothy and Margaret, and the younger Caroline and Constance. All of these sisters were attractive in various ways, and, according to rumour, Edward may have previously been attracted to both Margaret and Caroline; but narrowing the field in this respect was Margaret's marriage to one of Edward's closest friends, his fellow artist Frank Bennett. The latter, it is recalled, had made the trip with him to Italy.

Bennett specialized in fashion, flower, and tavern scenes; and among his accomplishments in later years was his contract with the Wills tobacco company to paint a cigarette card series entitled 'English Period Costumes'. Though he was keen to learn more of Edward's 'Venetian secret' technique, which Edward had no intention of divulging, both men remained friends throughout their lives; indeed they helped each other on many occasions, with not a little good-natured rivalry in vying for commissions whenever their painting interests crossed. With Frank Bennett's marriage to Margaret Pellew in August 1907, Edward must have been spurred that much more to follow his friend's example. But many obstacles stood in his path.

Bennett was an extremely popular and successful painter with his scenes of men smoking clay pipes and of monks playing chess, and he made enough money to sustain the matrimonial home. Edward was more diffuse with his pastoral landscapes, while his portraits tended to be more societal and less commercial. Because of this he probably earned less money than his friend, and, being cautious and reserved by nature, he was constrained to wait longer before he could ask for Anne's hand. It was one thing to be burning to marry, another to have the necessary means to accomplish this. There was also his conservative father to consider. One thing was sure: once he had made up his mind to get engaged, nothing – not thoughts of Dorothy, Caroline or Constance – would deter him from his choice.

Good news on behalf of his prospects had already come in 1904 with his successful exhibitions at the Carlton and Dudley Galleries, already mentioned. And surely an especially exciting moment came for Edward when he learnt that his painting *Annie* was to be hung in the Royal Academy exhibition the following summer. A few months later, in the autumn of 1905, Edward's *Milking Time* was included in an exhibition at the Grafton Gallery – a realistic

Milking time

tour de force depicting a milkmaid tending a close-packed herd of cows in the low, broad light of a Dorset evening, which he had worked at with exactitude and patience. 'The Autumn Exhibition at the Grafton Galleries', commented Vera Campbell in the *World*, 'is not an exhilarating one. There are many commonplace portraits . . . but praise can be given to Mr E.F. Wells's *Milking Time*, with its pleasant reminiscence of Richard Wilson's landscapes.' This view was endorsed by the *Standard*, which pointed out that the same work, 'low in tone, massive and dignified, owes much, and has a right to owe much, to our earlier English School.' The *Glasgow Herald* in its November review, pronounced the Grafton exhibition disappointing, but 'works by E.F. Wells [and others] stand out from a crowd of indifferent performances often on a large scale'. Other reviews said much the same.[6] Decades later *Milking Time* was bought by Mr Sydney Samuelson, who, with his wife Doris, proudly displayed it in a floodlit setting at their home.

The *Glasgow Herald*, among others, gave similar praise to Edward's drawings of the Downs and other scenes on display at the Royal Institute of Painters in Water Colours in March 1906;[7] and this was repeated with his more impressionistic *Cows in Meadow* amd other cattle scenes on exhibition at the Royal Institute of Oil Painters later that year. 'Mr E.F. Wells's honest cattle pieces', ran the *Glasgow Herald*, 'serve as a tonic as we go round.' 'Mr E.F. Wells and Mr F. Jackson have prompt little studies of cattle,' echoed the *Daily News*, 'close to impressions of sunlight and shadow.' Indeed, Edward's studies of cattle in hot sunshine or under the shade of trees were noticed by other publications, such as the *Western Press* and *Art Journal*.[8]

Nor was this all. In October 1906, possibly through the Ilchesters' contacts, Edward secured a commission to paint the Hon. Kitty Liddell, daughter of Lord and Lady Ravensworth of Ravensworth Castle, Gateshead, thus continuing a long list of portraits among county families. Then came more good news with the acceptance of both *Maggie, Guy and Joan, Children of Peter Ormrod Esq.* and a primrose scene called *Woodland* at the Royal Academy in 1907. And this triumph was followed by *A Wild Evening*, exhibited at the Royal Academy the following summer. The *Queen* had first noted Edward's Academy success with the acceptance of *Annie* back in 1905, and now with these 1907 exhibits *The Times* took up the theme of eulogy with its customary sedateness: 'There is a group of children and a pony by Mr E.F. Wells, which, so far as we can judge of a work unduly skied, appears to be treated with a certain originality.' As for *Woodland*, the *Glasgow Herald* referred to it as a 'well-constructed landscape study'.[9]

There had been disappointments in previous years – evidence suggests that his *Sandsfoot*, *Mimosa* and other paintings may have met with rejections – but sister Maud's congratulatory letter on his double triumph of 1907 went a long way to buoying everyone's spirit. She included a skittish poem:

Oh ye walls of yon Academy,
How celebrated must ye be!
Our hearts thus get rejoicing
When works are hung by thee.

Oh much abused mansion
By artists one & all,
Yet we hurry to accept
Thy varnishing re-call!

How honest are thy critics!
Valuing their opinion much
We long to give our pictures
Just the satisfactory touch.

Be careful of our humble canvas,
Place it not behind thy door
Or forget its poor existence
And leave it lying on the floor. . . .

Academicians & fair mesdames
We bow low to thy decree,
Faulters in word & action
We crave but praise of thee![10]

Congratulations poured in from all sides, not least from Anne; and with her love obviously responding to Edward's, some inkling of the artist's mood can be seen in the following letter he wrote to her later in 1907 while he was staying at Evershot:

. . . it's awfully sweet of you to go & get me a 'grip' but it's naughty of you to *spend* your money . . . really it's very wrong of you, . . . but of course it will be most useful particularly for carrying out wet panels, which are always such a nuisance. We had a splendid picnic on Wed.; glorious day & the colour up there was magnificent, with wonderful blooming blue shadows lingering on the distance, which was soft and misty. We tea'd in that beech wood just beyond the 2nd Badcombe gate (on way to Mintern) & just the other side of it there are two splendid subjects, one in the beech wood tumbling over the edge of the down into the distance, looking up sun in the evening with the gold misty light breaking over it all, it was glorious, enormous sense of space & light, & looking the other way there was a fine rolling piece of down breaking steeply to the distance, & the little bushes & trees clinging to its sides & then the great distance like a rippled sea. I longed for my paints but I had to play rounders which was rather amusing.

I managed to make quite a lot & got very hot running; it would have made you laugh to see Mr Whittaker playing & waddling after the ball! I *must* paint those subjects, superb, I wish you could have seen them; the conditions at that moment were perfect, & it's good to have seen them there. Yesterday we had a wet day & I worked in the studio; I think my waggon comes rather well in the Lewcombe; I made my studies in a cornfield where they were carrying. I've finished up the hay cart too. Today there's a great wind & torn clouds racing across the sky; I was out on Lewcombe trying to make a sketch this morn., but the wind was too much & the clouds lost their grandeur & became mere rags. I have just heard from Williams [John Williams of Scorrier, Cornwall].[11] He says he can't put me up till the 1st or 2nd wk. in Oct. as his boys are at home & wants me to go there then & will fix a date later. So darling will you come down here in Sept.; it seems already ages since I saw you & it's really a bare week! . . . Is the Admiral finished & how did Frank [Bennett] get on? Jolly for them going to Derbyshire, fine country I know. Is Frank commissioned to paint Haddon [Hall] or are they just going for a tour on their own acct.? . . . There's a great cricket match on here tomorrow against the fleet; we are lunching three of them. You seem to have been hard at work in the garden, which must be looking all the better for the rain . . . How's your voice, darling? I send you these roses, to add a sweetener to your own little room – if they survive.

With all my love my dear one,
Eddie[12]

Edward's curiosity about Frank's activities in Derbyshire, incidentally, reflects his own stay in the region of Haddon Hall two years before. Perhaps he feared that Frank would steal a march on him by getting commissions from the titled occupants of this seat. The fruit of Edward's earlier visit to the Derbyshire Peak District at any rate was his beautiful oil painting, *The Path to the Winnatts*, that points to what locals call 'The Shimmering Mountain' near Castleton and the famous Blue John caves. It was purchased for the Scheiwe collection in 1989.

If Derbyshire inspired him, then surely Dorset – with Anne at the centre of his thoughts – inspired him a great deal more. The foregoing letter is a full expression of this mood, its racing rural pulse typifying such works as *Milking Time* or *The Last Load* – the latter, incidentally, to be exhibited at the Royal Academy in 1912. Here was Edward scaling the peaks of his earlier professional life. With five showings at the Royal Academy to his credit by 1910, innumerable private exhibitions in such galleries as the Carlton and the Grafton, not to mention a number of portrait commissions, Edward felt he had won his spurs. Now was the time to lay bare to his parents his firm intention to marry.

But when Edward approached his father he was stunned to receive a firm rebuff. For all the good news of his Academy exhibitions, it was pointed out to him, this didn't mean money in the bank; and here it is worth quoting from one of the last letters the cautious Howley Wells ever wrote to his son. In it there is mention of Edward Gore Ring (Edward's maternal cousin), who met with a tragic accident – believed to be a fatal clawing by a wild animal – while on an African island. From this relative Edward Wells received a small legacy – smaller, as it turned out, than he imagined:

My very dear Eddie,
I should have written before, had I not been so unwell for some time with continual headache. Your mother showed me your letter re. your intended marriage when poor Edward's affairs are settled up. If she cannot persuade you & Anne P. to prudence, I do not suppose that I can hope to do so, whatever I feel in the matter myself. I can only trust that you may not act too hastily or that you will not arrange anything definite till you have discussed matters with me. I can understand this little legacy [from Edward Ring] turning your thoughts that way but you must remember that love is always depicted as blind to other matters beside itself. . . . You speak of £300 a year besides what you may earn but that will be more than the income of Edward's money at sound interest, *a great deal* unless you dip into capital by spending the full rents of the house in lease [in Church Row, Hampstead?]. Your legacy really capitalised is worth £4,000 *at most*, or £160 a year safely invested. Your prospects in the Profession are still, as you will allow, very precarious indeed & must be a cause of anxiety, & however good your work may be it has yet to be recognised. To risk the responsibilities of marriage & with heavy studio rent to be paid out on such small means certainly amounts to a gamble which in my opinion no one has a right to undertake. In a year or so's time you may find your prospects in your profession improving & at all events more warranty than now for marriage. Besides it seems to me too soon to irrevocably take from Edward's capital for your own, even though the chance of his reappearance seems hopeless. You have no doubt weighed all this, but with love in the balance, which is the handicapper, . . . I should not be doing my duty if I did not urge prudence & a little patience. In every way just now matters are in a precarious state with us all, worry financial & otherwise. In another year or so things may be looking up & your profession also. An imprudent marriage can only add to anxieties & possible further worries. Having said all we can, I can only leave the matter to your own good sense, & at all events trust that you will wait to talk matters over with me before anything definite is decided. I will write to you in a day or so about recent V.S. ['Venetian secret'] experiments which are more important & prove what I was discussing with you in London. I have been studying Joshua [Reynolds] a great deal, & feel sure of my ground now.
Yours affectionately.[13]

But Edward was determined to press on regardless. At whatever point he formally proposed, Anne was enraptured, and so was Edward's mother. As to Anne's family, her father had died in 1906, but the Pellews as a whole apparently approved.

Plans were already advancing for the marriage when a devastating blow was struck with the sudden death of William Howley himself. On 21 July 1909, he suffered a fatal stroke at the age of sixty-one while playing tennis at an Evershot garden party. Angina with cerebral haemorrhage had taken its toll. It was a blow in more ways than one. Not only did the event deeply affect Edward – his father after all had been the mentor who had encouraged so forcefully his search for a direction in painting – but it also meant that Edward's family had to leave Moorfields, the steward's house at Evershot where he had lived the greater part of his life. They moved for a while to 'Dartvale', in Ashburton, Devon, with which his mother had connections.

Despite the tragedy, there were compensations. One reason for Edward's long engagement to Anne, as we have seen, was the need to provide her with an adequate standard of living; and though he was making money from professional portraits, there were justifiable restraints on too hasty a wedding, as his father had clearly demonstrated. The latter's death removed these restraints, for adequate means were now left to him. He received about six-elevenths of the residual income from the trust his father had willed with his solicitors, Hardisty, Rhodes and Hardisty, his sister Maud receiving about five-elevenths. There was also the part share of a lease on a period house in Church Row, Hampstead, the other part being held by Edward B. Hardisty himself (who had sat to Edward and was related to his paternal grandmother, Jane Rose Fanny, née Hardisty, who was buried in Hampstead). In addition, there was the bequest from the deceased Edward Ring. Modest as all this was, Edward was free at last to discuss the wedding arrangements with Anne's family, speak his terms, and firmly tie the knot.

When it is realized that the rate of inflation in those days was much lower than today – Charles Dickens's salary of about £1,500 in 1840 as a reporter and writer could buy almost the same amount of goods and services in 1900 – Edward was fortunate enough with his legacy even at one third of the above figure. He thus caught the Indian summer of the pound's stability, for the approaching Great War of 1914–18 inflicted only partial damage.

His oncoming wedding, then, reflected his happily improved circumstances and they were duly married on 4 January 1910 in the parish church of Easthampstead in Berkshire. Edward had the satisfaction of knowing that both his parents in the end had given their prior blessing, for his mother, who had always kept on good terms with Anne, had most surely won round his father. The Wells family were henceforth related to the Pellews.

Edward's sister Maud was ecstatic. The following letter she wrote from Ashburton on the day of the wedding may sound amusingly Victorian, but she was to prove her worth later by getting a novel published, *Skim Milk*, a very down-to-earth unsentimental novel about Dorset life. Accompanying the letter was a bell-shaped tribute of flowers:

My darling Eddie & Annie,
Accept this little remembrance of the greatest & most solemn event in your lives – the birth of your Mate-Day. . . . My own brother, I am with you this morn – my eyes can see thee, my soul vibrates with thine. Annie dearest, let me hold you in my arms & call thee sister. . . . God grant to your pure soul peace and joy, now & always. Be happy, my dear ones. May each clang of these wedding bells beat down the ill luck & give birth to the good! The contents of this chime speak for themselves. The whole idea sprang upon me, & thus have I carried it out. Take it for what it is worth. The flowers will fade, but my basket and my efforts will remain created by the love of thy sister Maudie.[14]

Her remark that 'the flowers will fade', incidentally, had its prophetic endorsement in that the lovely manor house in Easthampstead where the reception was held fell into such a state of disrepair many years later that it was condemned by the local council!

But 1910 saw the married pair honeymooning in Corsica. Their mutual happiness goes without saying. The romantic, historic island inevitably inspired a sketch or two by Edward – the furtive inlets and bays with their little fishing boats still reflecting the undisturbed scene of centuries before the advent of tourists *en masse*. Believed to be of Corsica, incidentally, is a sea sketch signed by Edward (he didn't always sign his works at the time, much less date them), in which there is a tiny riddle. In the middle distance is what appears to be a perfectly proportioned sailboat, though whether this was done by design or by the subsequent accident of a chip on the canvas is unclear. Such mysteries abound in paintings.

Elsewhere on the island were other settings to delight the couple's eye. There were the quaint inns, more Italian than French, the fish piled high in ancient nets, the rich plants and vegetation, varying from citrus fruits to olive trees, or the valleys swathed in sunlight; and historic sites ranging from the one-time haunts of bandits to Napoleon's birthplace at Ajaccio. It was an idyllic time for Edward and his bride. Most delightful of all, perhaps, from the artist's point of view were the choppy seas with restless waves, the salty ozone one could sense even in the coves, the scrubby, sandy shoreline interlaced with brush. Here was the power of nature in the raw, with its loveliness, above all the joy of sharing it with another. For the first time since his Italian days, Edward was beholding nature when he wasn't alone.

On returning to England they went to live at 7 Rossetti Studios in Rossetti Gardens, close by Cheyne Walk and Flood Street in Chelsea, which Edward had rented since 1908. There was no shortage of work. He received a commision, for example, to paint the Reverend Harvey W.G. Thursby of

Norwich that summer. ('The picture looks quite charming and I am very pleased with it'), and he no doubt took the opportunity to paint scenes of Norfolk at the same time.[15] Two years later, in 1912, an exhibition at the Huddersfield Corporation Art Gallery included his Norfolk and Corsican scenes. The *Huddersfield Chronicle* singled out his *Early Morning, Norfolk* for special praise and otherwise commended his wide range of theme ('his varying subjects and effects are skilfully treated'); the *Huddersfield Examiner* said as much, with praise given also to the watercolours of Gerald Ackermann, whom Edward befriended and was to meet again in later life.[16] As for Edward's *Distant View of Ajaccio*, a legacy of his Corsica trip, this was bought outright by the Huddersfield Corporation after a showing of hands by keen councillors.

In London, meanwhile, evidence suggests that he was now working at oil portraiture rather than pastel, and continued to give exhibitions of works whose sale proved profitable to sponsor and artist alike. Trevelyan Turner, one of the original directors of the Carlton Gallery, had got into a financial mess some years before, but he continued sporadically as Edward's agent into the 1920s, while a happy outcome was the fact that Trevelyan's son William ('Willy Turner') became Edward's lifelong friend. As a later director of the Bernard Art Company Willy served Edward's interest in a number of ways, often including varnishing his work for various customers.

Demand for the artist's services was proving so great in fact that he and Anne found the Rossetti Studios simply too small to accommodate the work Edward was now doing. Thus in January 1911 they moved to a delightful period house in the heart of Chelsea – Cedar House, at 48 Glebe Place. Here two studios gave on to a tiny walled garden. Among subjects Edward painted in this pleasant spot was one of 'Nan' (as he now called his wife) holding their first child Judith, born in March 1911. Entitled *In a Chelsea Garden*, it ranks among Edward's more lyrical studies and is now part of the Scheiwe collection.[17]

Two more children followed Judith – Sylvia, born in January 1912, and William, born in June the following year. A delightful drawing of all three made by their father, incidentally, was reproduced and sent out as Christmas cards in later years. In the meantime Nan became the focus for Edward's inspiration as they communed for hours in their little garden at Cedar House. Copies of the *Daily Graphic*, with photoflashes of King George V or the Kaiser and their consorts dominating the front pages, lay idly about, reminding readers casually that the Edwardian era had passed. But there was no presentiment of war in those final spacious years; and it was during this time that he painted one of the most ambitious oil works in the whole of his career, completed in 1911. Together with *Repose*, described later, it is a landmark of successful endeavour in his world of symbolic realism.

The Shower of Gold, also called *Laburnum*, reveals a nude female figure lying under a laburnum tree (Nan having posed originally, before a model took

In a Chelsea Garden

over). In his interpretation of the legend of Danaë and the Shower of Gold, on which the painting is based, Edward replaced the golden mist (or coins) which Zeus poured upon the enchanting goddess with clusters of laburnum. The whole effect is a cascade of yellow and white. It not merely recalls the deeds of a pagan world from the past but some towering feat of nature, suggesting an artist with an instinctive sense of conveying permanence on a grand scale. The work appeared in the Royal Academy exhibition of 1911, where it caused a sufficient sensation for it to be parodied by the wags of *Punch*, whose sketch of it was dubbed *La Burn 'Em*.[18] Disguised flattery this surely was, for it was critically acclaimed by members of both public and press. The *Academy*, for example, wrote: 'Of a dazzling character . . . is *The Shower of Gold* by E.F. Wells, where laburnums droop over a nude girl lying asleep below the vivid bloom: the effect is superb, and very decorative.' The *View* took an equally praiseworthy stance: 'In [Gallery XI] notice . . . Mr Wells's *The Shower of Gold* (772), the sun pouring on the colour of the laburnum tree breaking into shadow on the nude figure stretched beneath.' The size of the canvas, occupying the best part of a wall 8 ft. high, reflected Edward's ambitions at the time. Besides, there were plenty of rooms in those days large enough to contain it. It was surely propitious that it was purchased in 1946 by the paper industrialist Mr Charles Pretzlick senior, who was also his sitter and whose love of art and ample resources would ensure its proper care. Mr and Mrs Pretzlick, besides their son Charles, had two beautiful daughters, Elfreda and Tilla, and after the latter married into the Scarsdale family, the painting came into the possession of Tilla, Viscountess Scarsdale, who lived at Kettleston Hall in Derbyshire.

The following year, 1912, another triumph came Edward's way with the acceptance of *The Last Load* by the Royal Academy for the exhibition of that season. Pastoral and realist in tone, this oil work focuses on the manual exertions of Dorset farmers at harvest time, who are shown building a stack, such as he had often seen around Evershot. It was sold many decades later to a dealer who had it destined for America, but its present location is unknown. Meanwhile a successful exhibition at Huddersfield, mentioned above, completed his main activities for this year.

With increased need for space and with increased expenses as there were now three children to bring up, Edward and Nan sought a larger, cheaper tenancy, and in October 1913 they again moved. This time it was Delcombe Manor at Milton Abbas in Dorset. It was offered to Wells by Sir Everard Alexander Hambro, a member of the well-known banking family, who, as a sitter, had long been an admirer of his work and whose house at Biarritz he was to sketch in the 1920s. Edward had in fact been at Delcombe before. The lease cost only £40 a year – a far cry from the £150 he had been paying in Chelsea. The nearby beautiful abbey, with its spacious parkland, tended plants and rose bushes, its grass steps leading to a Saxon chapel, and its wild bluebell woods sweeping back toward Delcombe Manor itself, was a paradise for any artist. Nan and the family were idyllically at home here too. There was even a Ford motor-car, the children revelling also in pack-saddle donkey rides close by. A hasty sketch of a group of choristers filing into the abbey for evensong, along with the exquisite *Bluebell Woods*, are just two samples of the tenor of the artist's mood. Indeed there were sources of inspiration all around, such as the beauty spot of Bulbarrow, where he touched off a number of brilliant watercolours.

Delcombe Manor was once a monks' retreat, and in an adjoining barn, which Edward used as a studio, little streaks of paint from his brushes bedaubed the walls. These queer relics intrigued many a subsequent guest at the manor, especially those who might have attributed such things to ghosts or messages from the dead!

Still at the peak of his creative power at Delcombe Manor, in 1914 Edward completed another nude study to supplement *The Shower of Gold*. Entitled *Repose*, it is a study in oil of Nan reclining on a daybed. It is a far cry from the *Annie* of Royal Academy success in 1905, or from any of the three other portraits he did of her. Comparable in subject matter (though not in style) with Velázquez's *Rokeby Venus* or Goya's *Naked Lady*, it yet breathes a life of its own – neither Spanish, baroque, roccoco nor like Renoir – but a work in its own right, with elements of Titian and Classical sensuality reborn in an English style. Though smaller than *The Shower of Gold*, the canvas attracted the attention of many critics and was well received. But it was in Ireland where perhaps it met with the most acclaim. Here Mr Dermot O'Brien, director of the Royal Hibernian Academy, approved its exhibition in Dublin that season, where it was greatly admired. The *Daily Express* of Dublin, for example, wrote: 'There is a clever and smoothly-painted nude study by Mr E.F. Wells, entitled *Repose* (No. 72)';[19] but this alone scarcely does justice to the verbal commendations by viewers that extended beyond the duration of the exhibition.

Regretfully, it was poorly restored on the Continent many years later, so that the patina and shine were rubbed off, diminishing the luminosity associated with the 'Venetian secret' technique which Edward had studied so closely. Leonardo da Vinci, whose own works have been even more disastrously handled, would have commiserated. So also would have Delacroix, who once wrote in his journal that 'every so-called restoration is an outrage, a thousand times more lamentable than any ravage wrought by time; it is not the picture which comes back to us but a new one, the work of the miserable dauber who has replaced the author of the original work which has disappeared under his brush.'[20] Wells's *Repose* is indeed a mournful illustration of this truism. (From a reverse perspective in terms of too bright colouring, so is also, according to some, the work of restoration going on in the Sistine Chapel.)

We may conclude with yet another *tour de force*. Completed in 1915, while Edward was still at Delcombe Manor, it is a magnificent Dorset landscape in oil. Strangely, it has two titles – *Wareham Heath* (some would call it *Egdon*

Wareham Heath, Dorset

Heath out of deference to Thomas Hardy), and the more cumbersome-sounding *Behind the Everlasting Arms*. Perhaps this is because there are two versions of the same subject – the larger one reproduced here, and a preliminary smaller one, now in the Scheiwe collection. They depict a wandering rustic, his wife and child seated on a horse in front, stoically crossing the heathland. Little streaks of fire in the distance impart a vivid sense of movement – from some encampment or perhaps the burning left-overs of a 'reddleman' or red-clay dealer, of a type described by Hardy in *The Return of the Native*. But in Edward's work the characters are dwarfed not so much by fate as by the contrast between the luminous overhanging sky at approaching sundown and the dark shadows which the clouds cast over the heath and by which the three figures are about to be engulfed. Humankind is here absorbed by nature in a single act, as dramatic in its way as the climax of an extended narrative.

Edward could now look back on his record with some satisfaction. There were his early pastel portraits shown at the Carlton Gallery, along with his later oil portraits, all of which earned generally favourable responses from his sitters – the Ilchesters, the Fullbrook-Leggatts and the Ravensworths among them. Some portraits known to exist, incidentally, have as yet no established dates for their completion – for example, those of Madame Bravet, the Hon. Agatha A. Fellowes and the Marchioness of Downshire (Ireland), to name but a few. And among the portraits of men, those of Sir William des Voeux and J. Wyndham-Smith may belong to this period or later. Be that as it may, his reputation was spreading, even among those who never sat for him. Captain Digby, Pamela Digby and Lady Lilian, for example, were very supportive (especially as Edward's sitter Lady Muriel, daughter of Lord and Lady Ilchester, had married into the Digby family of Cerne Abbas), while men-about-town like Leo Trevor, a relation of Lady Juliet Trevor, were lauding his work as 'quite delightful'. Moreover, Royal Academy acceptances aside, his watercolours on view at such places as the Dudley Gallery and the Modern Gallery, along with his fine cattle pieces at the Royal Institute of Oil Painters, all met with good reviews, as amply noted. The same applied to his later showings at the London Salon, the Bradford Municipal Art Gallery, and the Corporation Art Gallery of Worthing.

Many art centres of the time are today extinct. The Carlton Gallery, for example, where he exhibited many times from 1904 to 1908, and the Grafton Gallery, where his well-received *Milking Time* was shown in 1905, were eventually to become but faded memories, buried in the mists of redevelopment and takeovers. Yet London on the eve of the Great War remained much the same as it had been in the nineteenth century. It was still the age of large private houses, of plentiful domestics, of horses in the streets not yet being deemed oddities beside the motor-bus. But with the onset of the First World War in 1914 the English way of life was to be changed for ever.

CHAPTER FOUR

THE FIRST WORLD WAR AND TRAGEDY

With war service looming and with Nan in poor health and the children to look after, Edward had many problems to confront during this difficult period of his life. His painting took on a more restrictive dimension. Gone were the huge canvasses, making way for smaller watercolours, while the commissioned portraits, badly needed in order to replenish the family coffers, became rarer as wartime conditions took firm hold in England.

Already his Delcombe Manor days were over. In October 1916, his three-year lease having expired, he moved with his family to 7 North View, Wimbledon, which had belonged to his mother-in-law, Dorothy Mary. London seemed as safe a place as any. Everyone at first thought the war wouldn't be all that terrible. After all, wasn't this a volunteer army? So, despite the war's advance, Edward initially felt relaxed, with a number of successes to his credit – his brush, not a rifle, being his weapon of attack, dispensing brilliance with an easy-flowing style.

But things took an ominous turn almost as soon as he got to Wimbledon. Conscription had been mandated in January of this year (England was the last major combative nation in Europe to introduce it), and Edward had to join up early in November 1916. Patriot that he was, he knew he was no soldier and hoped that, as a man already turned forty, he'd be given only minor duties. There was little chance of avoiding military service in any case, short of registering as a conscientious objector. His mother's letter of 14 November, written from Minterne Parva, stiffened his resolve: 'You must try and think that you are doing a duty which must be done by someone and helps another man to leave England and fight for our very existence and all that we hold dear as a nation: no "world's applause" to be had for it, but to a conscientious man as you are, the applause of your conscience is more to be desired than medals.'[1] As if echoing these sentiments, Lloyd George, the prime minister, assisted by Arthur Balfour and Lord Robert Cecil, publicly resolved to prosecute the war with doubly renewed vigour now that Asquith's government had fallen.

It should be pointed out at this stage that the precise particulars of Edward's war service – of marginal interest anyway from the perspective of his art – are not known for sure, since his First World War records, as with those of so many others who served, were destroyed by bombing in the Second World War. We thus have to rely on his mother's letters for details, as well as Edward's own, though these are not dated by year.

The War Office appears to have requisitioned 7 North View, Wimbledon, or at least to have inspected it for this purpose, for his mother referred to this in a letter of 21 November 1916. Edward seems at first, however, to have settled down fairly comfortably here, engaged as he was in mainly clerical duties. He was permitted to do this apparently because of his age and anticipated 'C3' medical category, his mother even making the suggestion of his going into a munitions factory if he found his present work uncongenial: 'You mustn't allow the work to get on your nerves, dear. . . . You can't desert. You must back up the fellows in the trenches. . . .'[2] But events were moving ever more swiftly as the exigencies of war soaked up manpower fodder of every category. Though Edward qualified for non-general service as a result of a medical examination in early December 1916, it appears he was given a 'B1' category; according to his mother's letter written from Weymouth in 1917, this qualified him to join the British army abroad, including on the Western Front in France.[3] At this point his mother suggested he pursue a clever strategy. He must never shirk his duty, she insisted, but if the worst came to the worst, why not join the Artists' [Rifle] Corps, and train for a commission, but without actually accepting one when the time came? Gentlemen were increasingly going through the ranks anyway – she knew this personally from someone in the Tank Corps – so he needn't feel alienated in this respect. By forfeiting his commission he could keep his separation allowance for his wife and children, and would not even have to purchase his own outfit, whereas a new officer, with poor pay to begin with, would lose his allowance once he left the ranks. Whether Edward seriously adopted his mother's advice is doubtful, however; he never really aspired to a commission in the first place, nor did he receive one. We know he reported to Kingston Barracks in May 1917 after being downgraded from a 'B1' to 'C1' category by another medical examination that month, which virtually disqualified him from being posted abroad.[4] By the summer of 1917 he had been posted instead to Holt and Sheringham, in Norfolk; and evidence suggests that at some time, though the exact date is unknown, he was loaned or attached to the Artists' Rifles.

The following letter which he wrote to Nan while posted to Holt as a private soldier in 7th Platoon, B Company, of the 17th Essex Battalion, reveals his concern for his wife's safety after an air raid on London:

Darling Nan,
I got very anxious about you all when we had the report last night of the big raid over London, and was in hope there might have been a line from you this morn. to say whether you were all right. Do always just send me a card

on these occasions. The papers this morn. do not go into details as to the extent of damage but we hear its pretty bad. I hear a bomb dropped in Wimbledon Park? Did you hear or see anything of the raid? The planes did not come near here at all. I fear the aeroplane as a raider is much more effectual than the Zepp [Zeppelin] and more difficult to deal with. I wish you were not so near London. Nothing is yet settled about your coming down here . . . . Somerset Ho. don't keep the records of Indian births and suggest applying to the India Office, which I have just done. . . . Has Ritchie had the car? hope he brought it back safely! and saw to the oiling. Are the babes all fit and merry? I simply cannot get over being cut off from you all like this! It seems just like a nightmare. Have you been to any theatres or seen any pictures? It is still cold here in the E. wind. Have you got your coat and skirt yet? Much love, darling. Hope to hear tomorrow that you are all right. Don't forget to send me some card whenever there is a raid.

Your loving husband
Eddie[5]

Edward made contact with his family from time to time, probably from Norfolk, though one hastily-written note informed Nan that he couldn't see her and Mother for long on Sunday because of 'sentry go' the previous evening:

This Sentry business is a nuisance, as there's a lot of ceremonial drill to start with, and you then do 2 hrs 'on' and 4 hrs 'off' through the night in camp, until 6 next morning. Hope I shan't make a frightful mess of it! . . . Much love, darling. Hope to see you for a short time Sunday anyhow.
Your very loving E.[6]

That Edward was connected with the Artists' Rifles is suggested by the fact that the name of this corps appears on the reverse of the caricatures of the enemy he was instructed to depict on a series of small wood panels. The purpose of his task is best clarified in an unsigned and undated letter found among Edward's papers:

I draw attention to a very clever artist in Pte. Wells, 17 Essex Regt., who has painted in oil on wood a series of most villainous faces of German soldiers to be fixed on the top of the bayonet fighting sacks. The effect is lifelike and remarkable and from a psychological point of view undoubtedly valuable; I am sending 2 specimens to G.H.Q. for inspection. The head cost for material about 10 shillings a dozen.

Perhaps because of this, things took a turn for the better when he was posted back to London later in 1917. He seems to have alternated between his home at Wimbledon and the War Office at this time, engaged once more in mainly clerical duties.

Often chuckling at the memory of how his sketches of comic villainy drew praise from the right quarter (though they were probably completely useless in their effects on soldiers in actual combat), Edward many years later laughingly recounted some of his other Great War experience. On one occasion, while stationed in a transit camp, his fellow soldiers impressed him greatly in talking about 'pictures'. 'What enlightened men,' he thought, 'and how interested they are in the arts.' It was only later that he realized 'pictures' meant something very different – watching Charlie Chaplin on a screen, not dull, dry pictures on a wall!

But perhaps the biggest joke was the manner of Edward's own demobilization in that happy month of February 1919, when he was caught up in the vicissitudes of army bureaucracy. There was a minor railway strike (preliminary to the major one that September), and it had been snowing heavily, so that Edward was hard put to reach his demobilization centre at the London District Labour Office, near Moorgate, from his home in Wimbledon. 'I was too excited to sleep much,' he wrote to Nan, who was ill in hospital, '& got up soon after 4, got my breakfast . . . & left the house at ¼ to 6, with my old kitbag containing the oldest tunic & trous., pr. of boots & abett slung over my shoulder.' He managed to get a train to Waterloo and reached the centre via the Strand before 8 a.m., just in time to hand in his kit. But his problems were far from over. The NCO in charge had been given a railway warrant for the men to be taken to the next stage in the demobilization process, Wellington Barracks, and army red-tape demanded that they go by rail, strike or no strike. They took hours getting there, travelling by the Underground from Moorgate to Notting Hill Gate, and then marching four miles across Hyde Park ('We didn't half curse'), when a simple journey by War Department buses would have got them there much sooner. As a result they arrived too late at the barracks for their scheduled draft dispersal, and had to wait an hour for the next one. Leaving Victoria station at 12.15 p.m. they thought they were bound for Crystal Palace, but to Edward's agreeable surprise they alighted at Clapham Junction, and from there marched via Wandsworth to a camp in Wimbledon. ('The feed of stew & potatoes & beans was quite good, but there were no knives, forks or spoons! Of course a soldier is always supposed to have these things handy. Most of us, having been clerks for so long, had forgotten. Anyhow, I managed to scrape up quite a lot with a penknife & bread.') Edward arrived home a free gentleman at last, just in time for tea, though not without feeling sorry for many of the two hundred others in the draft dispersal who had to travel much further. The children greeted their father philosophically ('I'm not at all sure they didn't think him funnier as a soldier!') as Edward, having changed into his old green civilian suit, frantically searched for collar stud and spats.[7]

Another point of interest about army bureaucracy was the lax manner of the

War Office where Edward was sometimes on duty at night. Here he was surprised to learn that he did not need to bring the major in charge any incoming wires after 10 p.m., and so he could turn in. Any wires that came in later, the night porter was to hold and not deliver to Edward till the morning. 'What a farce,' as he rightly expressed it, 'Some day a really important wire will come in during the night, & there'll be a dust up!'[8]

But at least he had been spared being sent to the front. He had won no medals but he had done his bit for his country. The staggering list of casualties was best forgotten. And when the children greeted him, thinking him 'funnier as a soldier', his first impulse was to practise his skill again in wild, exhilarating freedom.

Inevitably it was his children who now increasingly received his attention. Of the three, it was William, a boy of five who appeared the most pliant model for his father's purpose, and *The Boy and the Apple* was the result. Attractive in his pink suit, eating a very red apple in a way Gainsborough might have approved of, William, with his shock of auburn hair and wild blue eyes, set against a dusky red background, made the painting an immediate success. It was purchased on its first showing at, it is believed, the Grosvenor Gallery, by a barrister named Mr Alan P. Mead. The popularity of the painting was such that Edward was urged to make copies, especially as one near-original was burnt in a fire. One such copy was later bought by a Mr Edwin Savitt of St John's Wood; while Katherine Wilcox, director of the Chester Gallery, requested photographic reproductions to meet demand.

William next obligingly stood in as Jesus in Edward's *Madonna and Child*, accompanied this time by the eight-year old Judith. Completed in 1919, the work was sent to St Peter's church in Hornsey, London, where it hung on one of the pillars in the nave. The Virgin Mary sits by a column in the picture, the child standing in front of her. Purple clematis is entwined around the column, the flowers forming the shape of a cross. This almost Pre-Raphaelite conception is one of the few purely religious pictures that Edward attempted. Reproductions of it were requested by admirers, including one Stephanie Cayley of Holly Lodge, Surrey, who wrote in July 1922: 'I was immensely struck with it. The face of the composite Madonna is extraordinarily beautiful, I think.'[9]

Leaving Wimbledon in September 1922, after visits to the Pyrenees and Switzerland (discussed later), Edward and family took a new house, 'St Margaret's', at 63 Beulah Hill, Norwood, in south London. Initially this gave them some months of happiness. The house was a neo-classic gem, with Palladian columns and acres of ground giving on to a magnificent view of Sydenham Hill and the Crystal Palace (destroyed by fire in 1936). This was indeed a prosperous time for those with even fairly modest means, for labour was still cheap, the pound still good, and the solid double-decker trams ran doggedly along their tracks for less than a penny a mile. Electric trains beneath overhead wires (known as the 'Elevated') rumbled out of Crystal

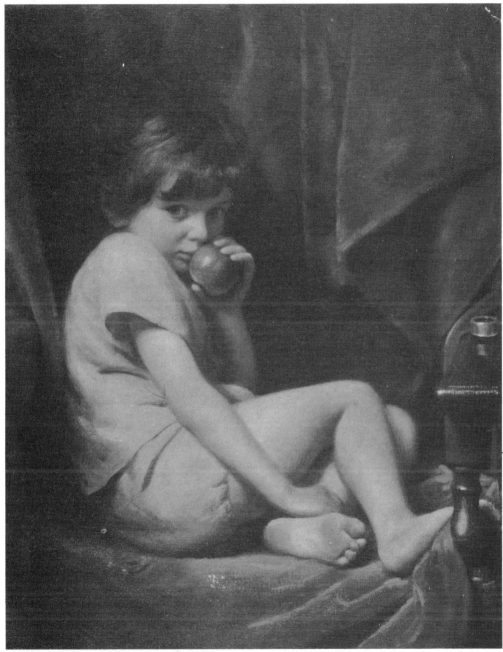

The Boy and the Apple

Madonna and Child

Palace station bound for Victoria, while Thomas Tilling petrol-electric buses could be seen struggling for speed through Peckham. The family came to rely on public transport, for Edward gave up his car – the only one he ever had – the old, battered Ford, first used at Delcombe Manor and Wimbledon, that had frequently blown clouds of steam around its radiator. William vividly remembered one such comic scene from a family trip to Weymouth.

In this age of comfortable illusions, meanwhile, when there would be no more war, no high taxes nor any inflation so long as a Bonar Law or a Baldwin were at the head of the government, Edward looked increasingly inwards. Nan for a long time had been having trouble with her lungs as the dreaded disease of consumption, or tuberculosis, slowly set in. Along with the children, he could only offer her what solace he could; and the house at Beulah Hill became a house of quiet melancholy, its occupants going through the motions, waiting for the dawn that could never really come.

But there were moments of delight along the way. Angelic William was not the only sitter for his father, and Edward's attractive daughters had their turn. In 1922, after their move from Wimbledon to Norwood, he painted the two girls, Judith and Sylvia, then aged eleven and ten respectively. By this time they had developed distinctive personalities and were like rays of sunshine in his life. He had already made sketches of them, including a delightful oil study of them posing under a rose arbour, probably at Delcombe Manor – the *Rose Arbour* was indeed its title – but this latest effort of 1922 brought out to the full their growing stature in a much larger composition. Dressed in white, they are sitting under a Japanese umbrella. They are shaded from the sun, the whole effect of the painting being a kaleidoscope of colour revolving through a spectrum of reflected light, suggesting the continuity of life no matter what cosmic interruption or human tragedy is there to disturb it. It is a large canvas, named appropriately *Children Under a Japanese Umbrella*, and Peter Scheiwe, the collector who bought it, prizes it as among the artist's most important works. It now adorns his home in Switzerland.

Edward's sitters from 1922 to 1924 included: Miss E. Cockett; Mrs E.E. Cox; Sibyl Longman ('In case I do not see you when you fetch the picture, I wanted just to send this line to say how very much my family like it . . .');[10] the Lushington family; and Lorna Pegg. He gives an interesting description of a professional engagement in a letter to his mother of 1923. He was to paint Lady Romayne Cecil, a daughter of the Marquis of Exeter, whose family seat was at Burghley House in Stamford, Lincolnshire:

I came down here on Wednesday, September 19th. This is a *huge* and most magnificent Elizabethan house (larger than Melbury) and full of pictures and art treasures of all sorts. Lord and Lady E. are most kind, and they have no guests which is a blessing. Lady Rowena [Romayne], who is my sitter, is a very charming little girl of eight and so good and pretty. I am painting her with her pom 'Cheeko'. I got a start with the picture on Thursday, and I think it is coming along all right, although I am only just beginning to get accustomed to my surroundings, which are always rather oppressive at first. I am doing a sort of Reynolds thing as that is what Lady E. wants apparently. They give me every facility – I am anxious to do a good picture, as it is to be amongst so many masterpieces. Most of the house is a sort of show place and is thrown open to the public on certain days. The grounds here are very pretty, but I fancy the country round is rather flat and uninteresting, although I have not seen it. . . .[11]

The letters to Nan were couched in the usual endearing and solicitous terms, but excerpts are quoted here chiefly to describe Edward's impressions of Burghley House and its occupants:

I have arrived safely. It certainly *was* a slow train! I got to King's X at 11.15 and found canvasses all right. A pony cart met me at the station, with a note from Lady E. saying she and Lord E. had had to use the cars to go to Peterboro' and that the butler would show me round, and Lady Rowena (my future sitter) the grounds. . . . This is an *enormous* house, most of it out of use I imagine. Lady Rowena (of 8 yrs.) has been in to see me; very attractive and all there, but quite simple and natural, quite a pretty child; she introduced me to her 2 dogs, Cheeko and Nulkin, a pom & a Norwich terrier. I understand the pom is destined for the picture; she introduced me also to a young Alsatian wolfhound, which was very shy. She hunts. Her young brother David is apparently off to Dartmouth to Navy school tomorrow. J & S [Judith and Sylvia] will be envious to hear that she hunts! It is raining, so we have been unable to go round the grounds as proposed. Lady E. is expected back to tea at 5. The country round looks exceedingly dull & uninteresting. The park is almost 11 miles round I hear. . . . *Much love* to you & the children, darling, do hope you will get on all right & not feel too bad.

Your loving Eddie

PS There seems to be *heaps* of pictures of [all] sorts in the house, but of course I only noticed them in passing. I should think it would take *days* to see it all. A vast barrack.[12]

He was delighted to get Anne's letters in exchange, which gave him a further chance to unwind:

Glad to get your letter yesterday. . . . The Exeters are nice & kind, especially Lady E. He rather reminds me of Bothwell to look at. This is a *huge* & most magnificent Elizabethan House, 1558. *Full* of fine pictures & things of all sorts. I have only seen a fraction of it as yet. . . . I have just been taken round the stables & grounds; lots of horses for all the children!

The stables and kitchens most picturesque. Even the kitchen has quite a fine picture of the interior of an ox hung up! We spent yesterday morning arranging a room for a studio & I got a start with the picture in the afternoon; the child is very good & a sweet little creature so amenable. Lady E. wants an '18th Century Reminiscence', so I am doing a Reynolds arrangement with her pom 'Cheeko' in! The start seems to be approved. Lady E. is quite knowing about pictures. . . . Lady E. has been much painted, there is a whole length by Ellis Roberts here & a bust by a man named Slocombe, which was given her as a wedding present. I advanced the picture today, but not as much as I should have liked as it was so stormy and dark this morning that one could hardly see; I did a bit more this afternoon. I suppose I am still suffering from strange & too magnificent surroundings, as I don't seem to be able to get absorbed in the work yet. I hope some spirit will return to me soon, as I feel one ought to produce something *worthy*! . . .[13]

The pom, 'Cheeko', incidentally, received a good smack from Edward when no one was looking, for not keeping still. Cheeko was so astounded at being treated in this way that the smack did the trick for the remainder of the sittings!
The next day he wrote to Nan:

Glad to get your 2nd letter yesterday. . . . The picture is coming on all right I think. The child generally comes for an hour, morning and aft., but her governess returned yesterday, so I am wondering how much I shall get in future. She does not sit very badly for a child, but somehow, unfortunately, I am not in very good fettle for painting; find it an effort to throw myself into it; I wish the mood would come upon me; it may be this house is too distracting! Lady E. took me round the show apartments yesterday, crowded with treasures of all descriptions; a lovely little Rembrandt of his mother, exquisitely finished; several Paolo Veronese, Albert Durer of St Eustace; a small Titian head. Queen Elizabeth's bed is there, a most magnificent affair. A Lord Burghley was her Treasurer & he used to stay here. The whole house is a perfect museum, I have never seen such a place. The Exeters are awfully nice & kind. The weather is very unsettled & I have hardly been out of the house; Stamford they say is well worth visiting, ancient buildings galore. . . . The Marquis has a wireless set, & I listened in with him on Thursday night. Last 2 nights I have been looking at books of Hogarth engravings, very interesting. I can't say I found the wireless very stimulating! Much love to you all.

Eddie[14]

He wrote again three days later:

My picture seems to be quite a success; the head is practically finished, &

everyone thinks it a good likeness of a very pretty picture! Also the pom 'Cheeko' has been finished today & causes raptures. A Lady Robyn who came to tea yesterday & was talking of pictures said she has just been staying with Lord Sandwich, who admired the modern French; she said they reminded her of *stamps*, which made me chuckle. I took her in to see mine & asked whether that was like a 'stamp'. "No," she said, "that's like a little girl," & she was very pleased with it; I am going out to dinner with her tomorrow to see her old pictures, as she seems to have some good ones. Rather nice of her to ask me; she wrote to Lady E. today asking me. A Lady Faulkner & children was over to lunch today, and was also full of praise of the picture; very pretty & just like the old pictures! The fact is all these people are just alike, they want 18th century reminiscences. Not encouraging for originality in the artist. I shan't bother to do another under the circs. Lady E. has found a lovely old carved frame for it amongst her spare ones. Charles II pattern & just suits it. The child is not sitting quite as well as she was; getting too used to me! & what with a restless dog & child I don't get things done as quickly as one might; about $\frac{1}{2}$ a sitting is spent in trying to get them into position! Not conducive to very good painting technically. I shan't be sorry when its *done* but can't say how much longer I shall be. The eldest daughter of 2nd son arrived late last night; very gay young people, who talk excitedly 60 to the dozen. The boy very good looking. She is quite jolly, but spoilt by specs. Also an old aunt of 74. . . . I get plenty [of sleep] here as breakfast is not till 9.30 & one turns in about 10.30 p.m. . . . I'm afraid I've missed the post tonight (goes out at 6) but tea was late & they have people there, so I couldn't get away. I spend most of the day at the picture, so between tea & dinner is the only time for writing. . . . Would you be very disappointed if I did not bring this picture back with me? I think I shall complete & leave it here as she has a frame, it seems hardly worth while. But I must say I should like to have had your opinion on it now. I seem to be in a curiously uncritical mood & hardly to know whether I am doing well or ill, & everyone being so pleased makes me afraid to adventure on a suggestion. . . . At the same time Lady E.'s eye has been trained to good & *finished* painting. Much love . . . to you & the smallies. Hope they are going to school happily. The tennis net ought to be brought in if it's not so already, and be *rolled* up when dry. I seem to have been here ages, I can't believe it's only a week today. I do feel this is a new connection which might be very useful to me if I can only do a *good* picture. I wish I was a better talker!

Your loving Eddie[15]

Upon the picture's completion, Edward's concern for perfect satisfaction was well expressed by his willingness to go back to Stamford to correct Lady Romayne's nose, which her mother had complained was too long – the only blemish, she wrote, in an otherwise perfect picture! Ten years later, when the

Lady Romayne Cecil

young Lady Romayne gave her coming-out party at 64 Rutland Gate in London, it was one of the grandest parties of the season. (Eight years beyond that, tragically, Burghley House suffered the effects of bombing in the Second World War, involving the loss of six hundred panes of glass!)

Infinitely more pressing for Edward than any portrait commission at this time was Nan's worsening health. Tuberculosis was taking its toll. And his letters reflect a helpless anxiety which no painting could assuage.[16] Even while he was still working at Burghley House Nan had been confined to bed. Back from his mission Edward would read to her and comfort her; and in this he was not alone. Family and friends rallied round in all sorts of ways. There were letters of concern from his mother, sister, and aunt, letters from Frederick Lutyens, visits from the Bennetts, visits from Frances, Lady Exmouth, and her daughter, and game sent up by the Ilchesters from Evershot.

Fearing the same dreaded disease was Anne's cousin, Edward Pownoll Pellew (the 8th Viscount Exmouth), whose family seat was at Canonteign in Devon. This cousin, along with his beautiful wife Frances, mentioned above, was not only well qualified to commiserate (he was a medical man himself), but in a more tangible way proved of inestimable help to Nan and Edward in their extremity. They helped to pay for Nan's private nurses, for example, and Frances in particular spurred others to contribute, despite Edward's protest at 'sending the hat round'.[17] They also recommended Edward's work to others. Earlier, they had invited the whole family to visit the Château de Bellevue in Jurançon, Pau, in the Pyrenees, where they had an estate and where it was hoped Nan's health would improve. It was certainly a paradise for the children. But though it was a fruitful time for Edward's painting there – his St Jean-de-Luz, besides Swiss, scenes were to go on display at the Chester Gallery off Eaton Square in 1924 – such an interlude did not result in Nan's recovery.

Nor did the trips made to Switzerland at various times. On medical advice Edward had taken her high into the mountains where she had rallied a bit; but as soon as they returned to England the symptoms reoccurred. This alternation took place more than once during the early 1920s in a steadily losing battle. On a hopeful trek to Arosa Edward relieved his concern with a brilliant watercolour of Arosa itself, besides others, and his painting with this title was hung in the Royal Academy in 1938, where it was sold, destined for Scotland.

Despite his brilliant scenes of the Pyrenees and Switzerland and their subsequent showings in London, he now lost the urge to paint. As Nan got progressively worse, medical opinions led by a Dr Swayne (who had sat to Edward) got likewise progressively gloomy. And Edward voiced this gloom in a letter to his mother: 'I know God is there & will help me spiritually. It's the material things that worry me; the ways & means. One wonders about one's children's future. But it is no use; one can only ask for help to face the daily things as they come, & remember that Shakespeare says, "Cowards die many times before their death."' It was certainly the 'ways and means' that were worrying him, for sickness in those days brought nothing but mounting medical bills. As Edward succinctly put it in this same letter, 'It's a "luxury" disease; if you have the money you can fight it.'[18]

As the months, the weeks and the days dragged on at Beulah Hill, Nan sought refuge in music, and in Edward's love and comfort. She died in his arms, calling his name, at the early age of forty-five. The year was 1924, in a sultry season, on that tragic, terrible date of 19 May.

The 'dark night of the soul' had come to Edward. Frances, Lady Exmouth, in particular stretched out her hand in friendship, helping him surmount his difficulties that spanned the 1920s. She would be there, in her correspondence, if not with physical presence, to encourage him with his exhibitions, such as a further one at the Chester Gallery in 1925 and a viewing of his Italian scenes later in the decade. Life had to go on.

As friends and relations poured in their condolences, perhaps some of them might have secretly thought that any of Nan's sisters, from fair Margaret to Caroline, would have made a better choice for Edward in the first place. But loyalty was one of Edward's characteristics. Nothing could have swerved him from his choice once it had been made. And it is clear they loved each other dearly. This was expressed in the many sketches he made of her to adorn their homes in Chelsea, at Delcombe Manor, Beulah Hill, and in their many letters. Perhaps the most telling record is a special study based on Nan's profile. He would always cherish it in her memory. The face is poetic, the pose uplifted slightly, eyes closed beneath the gossamer veil enshrouding her hair. The purple around her has a Pre-Raphaelite texture, a touch of calm assurance linking her with him in life, as now in death. It was a bond of deep spirituality as much as love – pure, unadulterated, almost pious. For this was how they truly felt.

Later entitled *The Sapphic Ode*, it is one of the most intimate, supremely personal efforts he ever made.

CHAPTER FIVE

THE YEARS BETWEEN

This was obviously a difficult period in Edward's life, concerned as he was with essentially family problems, and one can see this in his diaries. Not normally despondent, he was now in an emotionally unsettled state, his apprehension heightened by the prospect of having to face life as a single parent. Then there was the gloom affecting the children. They had spent many happy years when younger, and losing a mother in adolescence was a most grievous blow.

It was largely Edward's mother – 'Granny Wells' as she was called by the family – who came to the rescue. She left Bradford Peverell in Dorset, where she had been staying with her daughter Maud, and now joined her son's household at St Margaret's, their home on Beulah Hill. In helping with his affairs she was ably assisted by a good friend of the family named Blanche, who had tended Nan. There was also a housekeeper named Mrs Cadman – bent with responsibilities as she threaded her way through the passages laden with household wares and thoroughly worth her weight in gold by any standards. Other staff were on hand such as Mrs Moon. The household continued in this way for almost a decade, until Edward finally vacated St Margaret's.

His mother and Blanche, meanwhile, did a great deal to uplift the family spirits. The children needed extra care at so critical a time in their lives, and this supportive help took a big load off Edward's shoulders. The mother's personal attention in particular also sustained Edward himself. Highly efficient in household management and a keen observer of the political scene, 'Granny Wells' was indeed the matriarch of the family. She also had some financial means of her own inherited from the Gore Ring family, and took a keen interest in her son's professional life. Indeed, it was doubtless with her encouragement that Edward resumed his painting activity. This earned him money and relieved his mind of grief and brooding. Among his works, incidentally, is a fine portrait of 'Mother' herself, as she gazes placidly but commandingly, possibly in full view of the still rural fields. Years later, in 1988, the portrait was purchased by Mr Toshio Urabe, a retired Japanese diplomat, and made the long journey to Tokyo.

Already his style was changing, with less laboured detail, the outline more pronounced. Also he would sketch less in his notebook before committing himself to canvas – a sure sign of his growing confidence and maturity. Where watercolours were concerned, he had long learned to master the technique whereby he would wet the canvas and strike with paint just at the right moment, thus avoiding the pitfall of the amateur, who strikes straight on the dry paper, giving the work a stiff and lifeless look.

While his mother was unquestionably a strong influence in his life at home, as his father had been, Edward's great joy nonetheless was to get away for a while – beyond the lawn and the undulating meadows that tapered toward the Crystal Place – and to visit places further afield, such as Exmoor. He would tour the landscape, replete with watercolour paints and brushes as he had always done, seeking the perfect scene, the perfect inspiration.

But man cannot live by inspiration alone. And because of his skill and popularity with a certain kind of patron, he received innumerable commissions in the mid-1920s, many of them from county families. His connections with the Ilchesters, the Exmouths and the Exeters had not been for nothing. Impressive as this sounds, however, several portraits of this type were done by necessity rather than choice. An artist had to make a living, but in Edward's case his instincts were those of a wanderer, a seeker after beauty as he conceived it, not a seeker for social acclaim. Of county background himself, he lived by the code of his class but not by its creature habits. As such, he found it difficult to fit his artist's life into the mould of county gatherings. When he wasn't watercolouring, his greatest joy was to touch up old paintings, above all to cast new images of people with a sense of deep commitment towards the sitter. But outside his family there were few to whom he felt committed. Available as he was to the matriarchs and doyens of society, he was yet indifferent to the lure of endless house parties and to the formality of dress, being unaware, perhaps, amid all the gossip, of the eligibility of a widower. Neither did the hunt nor the shoot interest him. As a matter of fact he could hardly sit a horse, unlike his sister – a failing which had rather annoyed his father. There were indeed intelligent men and women with whom he had a close rapport – the Mallet family and Lord and Lady Forbes were examples – but in so many other cases the purely professional relationship was the measure of their interest in him, and he in them.

This is not to say he was without friends. On the contrary, while never gregarious, he had a small number of very close friends – Willy Turner, Frank Bennett, Vivian Rolt, to name but a few. But Edward was out of step with the relentless drive for prestige which the coveted RA status entailed. While willing to attend, say, the functions of the Chelsea Arts Club with its famous Ball, or the soirées of the National Art Collections Fund, he was at heart only interested in pursuing his vocation, willing in consequence to pay the price of isolation. To some extent this applied even to would-be patrons. As he had himself written in the letter already quoted: 'The fact is all these people are just alike, they want 18th century reminiscences. Not encouraging for originality in the artist.'[1] In essence he was fed up with doing 'pretty pictures', conceding that portraits could sometimes be a drudge and merely the wherewithal to make a living (distinct, of course, from subjects of special inspiration). All the time he longed to strike the open air – the scent of grass, the call of a bird, the pull of a cloud evoking in his mind the shapes of nature. In his deepest instincts he was a landscape painter first, a portraitist second.

None the less his list of patrons was impressive. In the mid-1920s this included: the Hon. Mrs Arbuthnot-Leslie and Lady A. Grant, both painted by Edward on a trip to the north of England; Lady Boyne and family; the Hon. Mrs Ailwyn Fellowes; Mr and Mrs Robert Harvey of Cornwall; Lady Marguerite Hastings and daughter; and the diplomat Sir Bernard Mallet and Lady Mallet (both personal friends of Edward), along with other family members such as E. Hugo and Victor. A specially lovable couple were Lord and Lady Forbes, of Castle Forbes, Aberdeenshire, who actually delivered their invitation by personal messenger. Part of Forbes's final letter to Edward reads: 'I must thank you again for the splendid portraits, which are a great joy to us. The rush of orders by the few who have so far seen them is the surest proof of your success.'[2] This was a correct assessment in view of the spate of commissions Edward received in the 1920s (names of other sitters are given near the end of this chapter).

Not all his commissions were by private recommendation, however. Lady Exeter may have praised Edward's work to Lady Hastings, Lady Boyne, and Lady Forbes, but other sitters could be introduced through promotion by an agent. In this respect, Trevelyan Turner appears to have surfaced once again. Edward never liked the idea of publicity agents – it went against his nature – but here he made an exception because of past associations and because of friendship with his son, Willy Turner. In any event, he could hardly refuse an offer when it came his way. Such was the case with the commission to paint Sir George and Lady Beaumont. On this occasion, however, things did not turn out so well as expected. Trevelyan Turner's letter speaks for itself:

> I have intended dropping you a line for some time with regard to Beaumont's portrait. . . . So far as the head is concerned I consider it finished but he says everybody remarks 'that it is not like his mouth and that he has a very long upper lip'; which as a matter of fact I consider you have given him. His hair may require a few touches and his coat and waistcoat and one hand require finishing. What is required to finish the picture should not take long, but before you come . . . I should give him to understand that you can only come for a week at most . . . and I think unless he gives you proper sittings you will not be able to complete the picture properly. . . .[3]

Annoying as this was to Edward – one cannot please everyone all the time – he nonetheless would do what was required of him. But he would not usually compromise over fees. These could approximate to fifty or more guineas for a standard head-and-shoulders 30 × 25 in. portrait.[4] In this respect Colonel John Williams of Scorrier reportedly urged Edward to hold his fees to the maximum, commenting that one horse-dealer told him he could always sell a horse more easily at an asking price of £150 than a mere £50! Even when Edward pursued this tactic, however, things could sometimes go wrong. On one occasion a wealthy and well-paying gentleman who was extremely fussy about his hair, necktie, posture and profile, suffered a blow to his vanity when his full-length portrait, so patiently worked on by Edward, suddenly collapsed from its hanging position when the wall-plugs gave way. The damage was repaired; but the artist smiled inwardly, ever so subtly, at seeing his sitter wince at the blows to the well-puffed visage!

Such mishaps however, including cases of dissatisfied patrons, were rare in Edward's experience. Praise would normally come in from all kinds of people, from places all over the world. Constance Layard (Nan's sister, and wife of Camville Layard), for example, commented from British Columbia, Canada: 'Cam., old Mrs Layard, & an old aunt think it is a splendid likeness & the expression & colouring very charming.' She goes on to mention that one person was so reduced to speechlessness over the portrait that all he could say was 'but it's so good, so good, you know, Mrs Layard; you see portraits which are so awful, but this is so good, *good*'.[5] Also from Canada (Winnipeg), a Madelaine Davis, in appreciating Edward's portraits of her children (Elizabeth and Margaret), wrote that an artist from Vancouver had painted about half a dozen portraits, mostly of children, the previous winter, and everyone agreed that Edward's portraits made those of this Vancouver artist look very crude. Indeed everywhere she went, people who had not seen Edward's portraits had heard how lovely they were and were asking to see them.[6] On the other side of the Pacific, at Rotorua in New Zealand, Mrs S.H. Hay (wife of Josie, who had sat to Edward) wrote about his portrait of their two children (Joan and Bubbles): 'When I first took it out of the case, I felt I wanted to ask the whole town to look at it.'[7] And from South Australia, Alex Melrose, a patron of long standing, frequently corresponded with Edward in appreciating his work. Some of his portraits, incidentally, were based on photographs, so that Edward frequently received acclaim for reproducing a likeness without ever having known or seen the person.[8]

After this spate of activity, Edward appeared to have slowed down somewhat by the end of the decade. Exhausting emotional problems, his reluctance to adapt his style to changing fashion, and his own advancing years no doubt contributed to this. Another problem was the need to provide for a still dependent family. Indeed his mother put it bluntly in 1931 when she wrote that 'our income seems diminishing year by year! Let us hope that it may take an upward turn before long, or we shall have very little left.'[9]

Perhaps this explains why, despite his sometimes relaxed attitude to business, Edward on occasions had to betray the values of his class by insisting that he get paid on time. A case in point concerned a portrait of an attractive lady whose husband said he couldn't afford to come up with the money. Edward responded by keeping the huge finished work in his studio until some sort of satisfaction was given – which, incidentally, it never was!

In regard to his family, there was William to educate, not to mention two blossoming daughters. Young William had already gone to preparatory school at Norfolk House in Beaconsfield, and at thirteen was sent to Bradfield Public School near Tring. For obvious reasons, it was a sad time for the boy; but as both he and his father realized, it was no good looking back. William, or 'Bill', as he was called, settled down and did well at Bradfield, as Edward had done at Clifton; and both son and father excelled in sports. During the holidays he loved to play tennis, or else table-tennis with his father in the library; and he perfected his French in Normandy after leaving school in about 1930.

Then there were the two daughters, Judith and Sylvia. Both studied at a convent near Norwood, which had the advantage of being close to home.

Drawing of my Three Children

Plate 1   *Self-portrait of the Artist at his Easel, c.* 1910

Plate 2   *Mrs W.H. Wells*, the artist's mother

Plate 3   *W.H. Wells*, the artist's father

Plate 4 *Maud,* the artist's sister

Plate 5 *Veronica Fullbrook-Leggatt*

Plate 6   *The Chalk Pit*

Plate 7   *Mimosa*

Plate 8   *Chrysanthemums*

Plate 9   *Return to the Cottage*

Plate 10 *Bluebell Wood*

Plate 11 *Cows in Meadow*

Plate 12   *The Blackmoor Vale*

Plate 13   *Corsica*

Plate 14   Nan, the artist's first wife (*The Sapphic Ode*)

Plate 15   *The Shower of Gold*

Plate 16 *The Rose Arbour*

Plate 17 Katharine, the artist's second wife (*Portrait of Kay*)

Plate 18   *Father Vincent McNabb, OP*

Plate 19   *Iris and Wistaria*

Plate 20   *Flowers on the Piano*

Plate 21   *The Seagull*

Plate 22   The author as a young man

Plate 23   *Mr Toshio Urabe*

Plate 24   *The young ballerina*

Plate 25. *Oxford oar*

Plate 26   *Mrs Doris Bowyer*

Plate 27   *Kay as a Dancer*

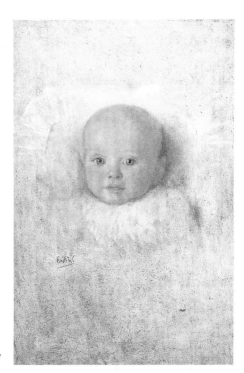

Plate 28   *A Baby Awakened*

Judith became sports-loving as she grew older, Sylvia more artistic and avant-garde. Judith, for example, joined the Norwood tennis club, where she often played with her father, while Sylvia by contrast preferred ballet, was a member of the Grotrian Music Society in her late teens, and studied piano under Tobias Mathay at the Royal College of Music. Both daughters, in fact, developed completely contrasting tastes; and this applied to their political views as well. Whereas Judith was a staunch conservative, Sylvia was left wing, and it is not surprising that the two girls parried on a number of occasions. In this the whole family would become good-naturedly involved. Sylvia for instance sported an artistic cape which annoyed Judith, and defended modern music, which annoyed Granny Wells. 'Up speaks the oracle,' Granny Wells would say, a bit sarcastically, whenever Sylvia held forth, barely concealing a growing preference for Judith; while Edward, a conservative in taste, would declare his strict neutrality by calling Sylvia his 'woodland nymph'.

Granny Wells had a good ear for music. No doubt she passed this on to Edward, who loved especially Bach, Handel, Beethoven, and any classical chamber work. She once made mention of listening to Bax and Isaacs, but had no sympathy for the 'squeak and squawk' school of music then in vogue. With Anton von Webern composing in Vienna, the generation gap was beginning to widen, Sylvia being definitely on the younger, modern side.

These brief details had some bearing on Edward's own situation. The three children demanded time, patience, and money. All three had above-average intelligence, and their needs were great, thus compounding the problem. It would be unjust to attribute to Edward a lack of interest in their lives. It was simply that by temperament and in virtue of his modest means, he was unable to fulfil the roles of two parents. He loved them deeply, if dispassionately. But even if he had been outpouring with his love, this would have made little difference where they were concerned. He could only go with them so far. Their directions were already being shaped, their lifestyles foreshadowed. What was needed most, as ever, was a mother's supportive role.

However, this predicament was relieved by two close family members who answered Edward's call – his sister Maud, and sister-in-law Caroline Pellew. Maud lived at Bradford Peverell, near Dorchester, with her husband Jack Crew Gee, who was a tenant farmer on a large estate. Jack, if at times morose, was a jolly, swashbuckling type, who joked of his descent from smugglers; and in the matter of his original elopement with Maud, when he was a groom at Evershot, he had run into real trouble with Edward's father, who disapproved of their courtship. But the marriage held, and Edward and his children had happy memories of their visits to Bradford Peverell. Maud, however, had enough problems bringing up her own large family. Her help therefore could only extend to providing Edward's children with attractive rural surroundings during their summer holidays.

For his part, Edward returned his sister's kindness by taking her manuscripts round to London publishers, from Cassells to Curtis Brown, following the success of her first book, *Skim Milk*, published by Arthur Stockwell. But family pressures and illness prevented Maud from repeating the above success, and on the expiration of their lease, Maud and Jack had to give up their farm at Bradford Peverell. They moved first to a rented farm near Wincanton, before finally ending up on a farm at Melksham, near Trowbridge, by the later 1930s. Edward's portrait of his sister when she was much younger, painted in the late 1890s, is now in the Peter Scheiwe collection.

As to his sister-in-law, Caroline Pellew (a portrait of whom by Edward has unfortunately perished), she now provided the help so badly needed. This especially applied to Bill. She took him under her wing, giving him the same degree of motherly love as Nan had given, and paying close attention to his education. This proved of great help to Edward, who was now relieved of much financial worry. But he rejected any notion of Caroline replacing Nan in his own life. Because of her strong supportive role, however, Bill found himself at St Andrew's University in the early 1930s. Here he excelled in tennis, completed his degree and afterwards wrote a scholarly monograph on William Blake. At his graduation Edward painted a portrait (which, alas, has perished) of him magnificently clad in the traditional red gown of St Andrew's. Indeed, while carefully concealing the fact, Edward was immensely proud of his son's striking appearance and intellectual gifts.

As the influence of Granny Wells receded with her advancing years, that of Caroline grew stronger. Politically, the two women were poles apart. Granny Wells would largely blame the Socialists for her steadily shrinking fortunes, while Caroline would revel in materialism and atheism, giving praise to Beatrice and Sydney Webb's *Soviet Communism: A New Civilization*. She was employed as a geneticist at the John Innes Horticultural Institute, then located at Merton in south London, where she assisted Professor W.D. Bateson (whose portrait Edward subsequently drew) and where she was joined by a close colleague named Mrs Caley, or 'Tools'. It is possible to infer from all this that Caroline had a particular influence on Sylvia, who was soon to change the course of her life.

It was the age of Ramsay MacDonald, whose brief Socialist regime at the height of the Depression (an even bigger crisis than the General Strike of 1926) led to the formation of the National Government in 1931. And it was Edward's mother especially who saw in these upheavals a reflection of her own situation. Astute and observant, she could comment with insight on many political figures of the day, from Lloyd George to Snowdon, Baldwin or Beaverbrook. And she could do the same with literary figures such as Aldous Huxley. She had a deeper grasp of reality than to waste her time grumbling about money, as ageing folk considerably richer than herself were wont to do. She died the next year in her eighties, a gracious lady to the end and mourned by more than just the immediate members of her family.

It would be superfluous to describe the effect this new blow had upon Edward and the problems which this personal loss brought to the running of his home. Fortunately Judith, Sylvia and Bill, now in their twenties, were becoming old enough to look after themselves. When down from St Andrew's during vacations, Bill increasingly stayed with 'Aunt' Caroline (whom he dubbed 'Tinto', a corruption of *Tante*) at her home in Merton, and later in Cambridge. The daughters too were launching out on their own. Judith was an active, as well as attractive, product of Norwood society by the 1930s – a girl pleasant to be with, full of fun, and intelligently feminine. It was not surprising that young men courted her. The winner was a businessman named Jack Train, who deftly swung her round the dance floor and skating rink, and in the end they were married. It proved to be an extremely happy union. Edward himself, of course, was delighted, though sorry to see his daughter go abroad. They emigrated to South Africa, where the young couple set up in fruit-farming and where Mr Train later forged closer trade ties with England, for which he was awarded an OBE.

Edward was equally sorry to see his other daughter go abroad when she emigrated to Russia in 1937. Sylvia the Communist was thus at odds with Judith the capitalist; and when they met over forty years later in England, with their father long gone, they clashed in lively debate, though without effacing fond memories of shared sisterly experience.

With his children leaving home, meanwhile, Edward had no more reason to keep up the house on Beulah Hill, and he finally sold St Margaret's in 1933. The colonnaded terrace and the beautiful grounds became faded memories; and, like the original Crystal Palace near by, the house has long vanished. To take his mind off things Edward travelled a great deal in Britain, touching off one watercolour after another as he roamed the land. It was here among its hues and pastures where his spirit felt closest to home. By September 1934 we see him in Scotland at St Andrew's on a visit to Bill. During this time he stayed at the Loch Ericht hotel in Dalwhinnie, Invernesshire, where he could look out across the moors and do some sketching. Braving the cold landscape on more than one occasion, he would set down his easel and paints to capture many a scene flecked with heather, lined with hidden grouse. Among the works he painted here was a watercolour of a stone bridge spanning a valley. It is a study of nature and man in perfect unison – the purple waters alive beneath the bridge itself, stone-faced, gaunt and grey like the bleak hills it connects. 'It breathes. It's all pure harmony. You never tire of looking at it,' are the comments of its present-day owner, a Miss Ingrid Horst, who lives in East Bridgewater, Massachusetts, USA.[10] Edward would have relished these comments, for he once recalled that he had never felt so cold in all his life! Another scene he did of Dalwhinnie, incidentally, was subsequently purchased by a Mr A. Labouchère.

Edward's old friend since their Carlton Gallery days, Willy Turner, was in touch with him in Scotland and suggested he join him in Hampstead in north-west London. Thus it was largely due to Turner's arrangements that Edward found himself staying at a guest-house here later this year. Gone were the expenses of running a private home, and he found the hotel atmosphere, with rest and quiet, a better alternative to the chores of domestic care. He was also lucky to have sufficient income, not to mention a studio to store his paintings. This was in Tatchbrook Street, Westminster, which he had rented for some years at a cost of only £8 a quarter.

To conclude this chapter, further sitters for portraits during this period of Edward's life, other than those already mentioned, are here listed: Lord Aberdare (of 83 Eaton Place, London), who wrote an appreciative letter; George Brann (secretary of the Home Park Golf Club, Hampton Wick, and a keen cricketer); Trevor Davis; Mrs Blanche Dickenson; Mr and Mrs R. Ingram's daughter; Mrs Bessie Marriott (wife of Charles Marriott, both close friends of Edward who also knew 'Alastor' and Willy Turner's family); the beautiful Frances (wife of Edward, Lord Exmouth, of the Pellew family); Violet Fleetwood Pellew; Mr Platt (husband of Florence Platt); Mrs A. Seabright; Mrs Arthur Selingly; and Major and Mrs Treffry. Most of these portraits were painted between 1927 and 1931. Dates have not been determined, however, for the portraits of the following: Miss Charlton; Monsieur Dessousier (son of the famous Parisian jeweller); Mrs Farquarson; the Hon. Mrs Mark Hovell; Lady Newport; Sir William des Voeux; and J. Wyndham-Smith.[11] All kinds of people are represented here – society ladies, sportsmen, businessmen – those to be found in manor, club, or office, and lending to the artist's eye a certain dignity and charm. Edward infused new life into a dying age of elegance.

He did so with authority. He had studied the Old Masters and learnt how to make their techniques serve his own purpose. His knowledge here was great. He looked backwards rather than forwards; and if he can be criticized for this, it can be said on his behalf that he looked back purposefully, so that the past, the best of the past, could reflect into the future. When painting on his own terms (not just doing a 'pretty picture'), he left a stamp of realism that was an authentic mark of his time. Characterization, not abstraction, was his forté.

Perhaps observation in all the senses of the term was his strongest point. In a junk shop in Norwood he once bought for one guinea something that passed for an old piece of linoleum with a seemingly unimportant figure daubed across it. But Edward knew better. As he rolled back one corner and scrutinized it closely when he got home, he observed amid the mishmash the outline of a sandalled Roman foot. But the canvas was laid aside and soon forgotten. Years later, long after his death and thanks to the persistence of his second wife, a team of experts pieced together the shreds of the tattered canvas bit by bit, and what turned out to be a priceless work now hangs in the City of Bristol Art Gallery. It is *The Rape of the Sabine Women* by Luca Giordano.

CHAPTER SIX

A NEW LIFE BEGINS

Katharine, who was to become Edward's second wife, was a very different personality from Nan. She was first introduced to him by Willy Turner in Hampstead in 1935, when she was thirty-four years old. Edward took to her from the start. Indeed, as the months passed, his invitations grew more pressing until the point was reached when he would hardly let her out of his sight. It was a harmonious meeting of minds in the world of the arts – of music, dancing, and literature as well as painting – in which an older man found close companionship with a younger woman. 'Beauty is in the eye of the beholder,' he once intoned, holding fast to the cliché, as if rebutting any challenge to this truism.

Nan and Katharine, then, were his two great loves – the former a fair tendril on the vine, giving her best in a tradition of solid, permanent values, the latter a fiery, headstrong personality, with a nervous energy new in Edward's life. Katharine's qualities were extreme, abounding with perhaps a bit too much self-confidence, but at least in respect of her passionate sincerity and admiration of his art she struck a chord in Edward, reminding him of his earlier days with Nan. In everything else, his two wives were totally unalike. If the term fretful could possibly be applied to his first one, the term reckless could be applied to the second.

The following excerpts tell all in regard to his feelings for his second wife; the letters were the first he ever wrote to her, but they convey a sense of commitment which lasted till the end of his life:

I shall this morning feel . . . glad to bathe in quiet absorption of nature's peace. Darling I wish you were here [in Bradford Peverell]. . . . Funny, this is the *1st* letter I have written to you. I feel a commotion of feelings which I have no means to express – inside me – for you. . . . The air is quite cool here, last night & this morning early, almost cold; the sort of thing one expects later in the autumn. (You would have felt the wind cold to your shoulders last night) but it's pleasant & fresh to have it so, after the close heat in London! God, how I wish you were here. . . . It would be nice to share the earth with you for a time & see you blossom as a Flower. I want to send you some wild flowers, perhaps I shall . . . . Well, here's lunch & my pen has run out – unaccustomed to so many words! I commend you to God's care, & – in thought – press your sweet lips. . . . Write to me.

Eddie[1]

And again:

> . . . Never can I forget how you came dancing out of the blue with your youth & beauty, stealing my old heart from me; it makes me feel overwhelmed that you should have given your young heart to an old fellow like me. . . . Darling, you have all of me, my heart's love.

Eddie[2]

Katharine was born Kathleen Ormsby Stather Dunn in London in February 1901, just missing the death of Queen Victoria by a few weeks. Her mother was the beautiful Constance Hardinge, who had been bilked of her fortune by a crooked trustee out in India. Her father was Harry Stather Dunn, a handsome scion of a Gloucestershire family from Woodchester, who had served with the British army in India. He had had much better luck there than Constance; one of his greatest achievements was to obtain permission from the viceroy to allow a certain maharajah on special occasions to fire more than the prescribed number of guns. Resigning his commission soon after his return to England, he made a considerable sum of money negotiating the sale to a film company of some land near Brighton. His handsome, bronzed face and winning ways, however, far from bringing solace and comfort to his family only brought disruption and hardship, for his life was one of irresponsible ease to the point where no one knew what he was going to do next. He once quipped that only three families were worth anything at all – the Holy Family, the royal family, and the Dunn family. While this very much impressed the children, who held their father in awe, his wayward conduct caused great distress to his wife, who tragically died of pleurisy in a London hospital in 1918, when she was barely forty-eight.

Constance's death was a traumatic shock to the three surviving children. Where Katharine was concerned, evacuated to England from Belgium when the First World War started, it radically changed her mental outlook. In passing from the very strictest upbringing in her Belgian convent to less settled ways in wartime England, she allowed her liberated emotions to suppress in her the socially conforming young lady she might have become; and in the process she displayed not a little of the haughtiness inherited from her father.

But her wilfulness got its results. Spurning the protection offered by those who could have introduced her into society, such as Lady Bute, she plunged into intensive ballet training at Madame Vandyck's Academy, near Swiss

Cottage, in London, the Ludicke family who lived nearby taking her under their wing. Here she performed outstandingly. By 1920, she found herself prima ballerina in the Carl Rosa Opera company, having been chosen by Princess Astafieva, who arranged the ballets; and next year in America she was introduced by Morris Guest to the Broadway stage. Great success, even fame, was now beckoning.

It is difficult to tell what deflected her from her career so sharply, but in all likelihood it was sheer homesickness for England. At all events, whereas most other people in her position might never have turned their backs on such an opportunity, she returned to London. Despite her Belgian upbringing and success in New York, Katharine always remained a Londoner by birth and instinct. Her nostalgia here was strong (unlike her sister, who settled permanently in America). Unfortunately, she was soon caught up in an unsuccessful marriage in which a son named Anthony Frederick was born, of whom she was very fond. Her debut on the world stage of life was like a meteor that vanished before its time. But the experience at least equipped her to cope with life's demands. She had a lot going in her favour. With her lively brown eyes, 'wild rose' complexion, dark auburn hair and a fine speaking voice, she attracted many friends. People were also impressed by her piano-playing at professional level (she had won a diploma in Brussels at the age of twelve), and by her knowledge of ballet and grand opera. She knew some of the scores page by page.

As to her faults, Edward must have been aware of them before his marriage, but they would not have deterred him. She could be impulsive at times, critical of others, and had a quick temper when crossed. While extremely generous, on the other hand, she could be over-extravagant whenever money came her way. 'A pound in Kathleen's purse would vanish like water,' as one friend put it, referring not to the pound of today but the guinea of the 1920s.

It was a second marriage for both of them when the knot was tied in a Hampstead registry office on 18 September, 1935. It was the Silver Jubilee year for King George V and Queen Mary, whose procession they had watched that summer. Perhaps they saw the stability of a royal commitment reflected in their own. Their marriage was certainly a success. Edward's tepid Anglicanism and the 'hell-fire' brand of Catholicism instilled in Katharine since childhood never clashed in the presence of their love, which served if anything to extinguish religiosity in both.

Edward's idea of God had in fact mellowed considerably since his youth. He held primarily to a notion of divinity in nature – in nuances of cloud, woodlands, skies, water and mist. His was an idyllic world as much removed from the niceties of theology as from the grime and squalor of industrialized England. 'We are all sons of God,' he once intoned, with a vaguely anti-Trinitarian, almost Hindu, conviction, adding that we should strive to see perfection even in an insect, 'lest it sink upon the waves'. He was quoting from an Indian poem. Edward still had fleeting memories of the Indian presence in his background.

As for Katharine, she shared his broad-based views largely because of her own cosmopolitan experience. Though both were a bit impractical, they had essentially a vital, poetic, attitude to life that was never dogmatic. She kept in touch with her co-religionists, however. One of these was Father Vincent McNabb, OP, the famous preacher from St Dominic's Priory in Hampstead whom she had known for a long time. Two years later she persuaded him to sit for a portrait in their new house in Parkhill Road, just across from the Priory, he commenting as he did so, 'Who wants my ugly old face!' But Edward's portrait of him was a success. It shows a man of consummate charity and meditation done with an encompassing skill in what must have been Edward's first contact with a mendicant friar. There was no evil here, as with some portraits of monks. Only godliness, humility, with a little self-mortification thrown in – qualities which Edward himself might well have appreciated after his own hard knocks of experience. Yet, on the other hand, he painted a much earlier portrait of a monk with a lustful, sinister expression – a shaven, monkish face shadowed by a red cowl – which dates back to his student modelling days at the Academy. It was bought by a Mr Michael Carol in the 1960s.

Edward and Katharine lived at first in a furnished flat, also near St Dominic's, at 66 Parkhill Road – still standing fifty years later. From the outset Edward warmed to his wife's highly-strung temperament, which he took for granted, as if this was the stuff of which true love was made. For her part, 'Kay', as he now called her, threw herself wholeheartedly into his world. Since there were no children by this marriage, her interest could be total.

At one of their early meetings, upon being asked what he did for a living, Edward replied, 'I paint a bit.' But this hardly described the galaxy of paintings hidden in his studio in Tatchbrook Street. Here scenes of every description lay huddled in their dozens, some on the floor, some turned to the wall, a few of them framed – portraits, landscapes, seascapes, flower paintings, still lifes – all excelling in design, a plethora of fine work. In the centre of the studio, an easel held the big canvas of reclining Nan – the *Repose* already referred to, painted when Edward was at Delcombe Manor. Kay must have been deeply impressed by this lucid reminder of his past. Its luminous texture in the half-light made her wonder why so fine a work had been left neglected for so long. As for Edward, one can imagine him feeling a bit strange at one wife learning more about the other in this secret hideaway.

Almost daily Edward and Kay now made the winding journey through September mists to the studio – first Victoria station, then down Belgrave Street and around the corner to Tatchbrook Street along to No. 149 at the end. There one could see the paved stones, the steps leading up to the front door with its old-fashioned pull bell and the studio beyond. Along the way they would pick up a bundle of wood from an oil store with which to fuel the coke-burning stove inside. It was a job to light: but once done, it soon warmed the dusty surface of each canvas, the smell of crackling wood blending with the scent of turpentine. They spent long hours together – no doubt nostalgically for Edward, as the glow from the heated stove rekindled memories of the past. But his companion also conveyed to him a sense of re-awakening to a new life, a new excitement different from the past. There could be no turning back.

Edward was in fact now approaching the second peak of his creativity. And the year of 1936 marks what is perhaps the greatest head-and-shoulders portrait in the whole of his career. Titled simply *Portrait of My Wife* or *Portrait of Kay*, it was completed in their flat at 66 Parkhill Road just before their move in April to their new home on the same street. It depicts Kay in a low-cut black dress – eyes penetrating, complexion rose-white, nose aquiline, lips compressed – as, looking straight ahead, she holds a cigarette in her right hand. Her strongest characteristics – the restless energy, the fiery personality, her excitement at living – all fuse in that one tense expression, which by its very tenseness arouses curiosity in the viewer along with compelling attention. It is no ordinary pose. Here is no study of mindless beauty in the delicately charged texture, but of strong intellectual passion. In the depth of concentration with which Edward painted her the outcome is a transmutation of this depth, masking the long hours of effort he went through, and binding both sitter and viewer to witness an extremely powerful portrait. For Edward in a personal sense it was an act of love, a dedication to a new commitment.

They had spent a brief holiday at Worthing in Sussex, with an aunt of Katharine, Lilian Plunkett, joining them, but now it was time for a more ambitious trip, and Paris was chosen. It was a belated, but fun-filled honeymoon that year of 1936. Here in the Louvre, in Montmartre, or by the Sacré Coeur, along the Champs-Elysées, or wandering by the Seine on the fringes of the Latin Quarter, Edward would savour the atmosphere of Paris, liking Monet, Degas and the Impressionists, but casting disapproving eyes at most of the work by exponents of cubism or surrealism, and other, more recent 'moderns', sensing (probably rightly) that some of them might one day overplay their hands. They visited the Eiffel Tower, the *Folies-Bergère*, and, of course, Versailles. In one of his more whimsical moments Edward turned to Kay and asked her, 'How would *you* like to have been one of Louis XIV's mistresses, eh?'

Returning to London, they were pleased to have finished dusting and assembling the paintings in Edward's studio, and had them moved to their new home. This was a leased Victorian house at 39 Parkhill Road, near their original flat. Long demolished, this house was occupied by them for eight years from 1936 to 1944, with the exception of brief periods on vacations. Primrose Hill and Hampstead Heath were within walking distance. Edward had been in hotels long enough – he had been seeking a new direction – while Kay, rent by conflicting ambitions and with a son to educate, now found

Katharine, the artist's second wife (*Portrait of Kay*)

herself with a kind, accommodating husband. It was the first big house she ever had. The walls were whitewashed, a Hagspiel grand piano came with the furniture, Edward's studio was made ready with easel, palette, and brushes. Chains and wires were adjusted to accommodate the huge canvasses on picture rails. Soon the contents of the studio in Tatchbrook Street filled the rooms and stairways of the house in Parkhill Road.

To understand the full effect these pictures lent to the viewer, something needs to be said about the different kinds of frame in use at the time. In the last century artists increasingly designed their own frames with the idea of adding to the overall aesthetic effect. Pomegranate motifs, ornate mouldings and borders, even fluted pilasters, were all in fashion, as if forming part of the dimensions of the canvas itself.[3] And much of this ornateness persisted well into the twentieth century. Where Edward was concerned, he often had determined ideas of his own. Thus *The Shower of Gold* had the traditional gold leaf ornamental type of frame in keeping with the style of the period, while his *Portrait of Kay* had the classic swept pattern. Even while painting for others, when he was obliged to consult with his patrons as to the suitability of a frame, the decision was largely his. Father McNabb's portrait, for example, had the luxury of a *Carlo Muratti*, while another portrait might have a Wilson. As every artist knows, there is a definite link between the expression of a face and the sensual dimensions in colour and design imparted by the frame. In short, the frame adds to the decorative effect, often reinforcing the message of the painting itself. As such, artists in general feel they have a right to a say in choosing what style would be best suited for the picture; and Edward was no exception.

Ornate frames abounded in their house. This was in keeping with its tone – solid and traditional, well supplied with classic furniture. It was a burst of grand living in the old style. There was a large kitchen basement replete with anthracite stove, scullery and cellars, outside which, at regular intervals, the coalman with his lumbering horse-drawn cart from Kentish Town would cry out 'Quality!' (meaning coal at half a crown per bag, and joining the lavender lady and the rag-and-bone merchant as among the last street-criers of London). There were barrel-organ grinders and knife grinders, aproned errand boys, steam-driven lorries chugging the length of Parkhill Road, men still begging for food or work. Hand-pulled bells seemed to ring everywhere – those from nearby St Dominic's Priory among them – as the Wall's ice-cream cart's tinkle joined the front-door bell, which maid or char would trundle up the stairs to answer.

Among their staff at No. 39 there was the impeccable Olive, paragon of maids, along with her handyman husband. And the less impeccable Mrs Bagshaw from Ireland, handling with equal dexterity packets of Gallaher cigarettes and filched packets of butter and sugar for hiding in her shopping-bag. But she was a lovable character all the same. Outside in the garden, a marble bust of Alexander Pope by Nollekens looked down benignly from the top of the steps on to the dining-room table below, groaning with good food always, including a bottle of Burgundy with every nightly dinner.

The routine of their lives thus established, they drew ever closer, reinforced by Kay's commitment to help promote Edward's work both now and in the future. She was there to share his interests, take part in his affairs, both professional and personal – urging, planning and organizing exhibitions of his works to the point where she became indispensable to his needs. Edward felt gratitude on this account. He indulged her every wish, forgiving her extravagance because she had given him new zest for life itself. And despite the generation gap, whenever they seemed to disagree on a topic, Edward would shift his ground markedly, as if conjugal love took priority over conviction – a sure sign that it was a marriage destined to last.

These years, then, were among the happiest in Edward's life. Only his youth and earliest time with Nan could rival them. It was a tragedy that both his marriages had to precede the oncoming of war. But little attention was paid by anyone to the newly impending threat; it was domestic events that mainly dominated the headlines. People were more interested in Edward VIII's abdication and George VI's coronation, though overseas, the Spanish Civil War, the Paris Exposition, and the wreck of the airship Hindenburg at Lakehurst, New Jersey, in May 1937 ('"Sabotage," says Dr Eckener,' ran the headline in the *Evening Standard*) raised flickers of interest. Not until the Munich crisis of September 1938, when Chamberlain went to meet Hitler, did people in Britain begin to wake up.

So there was time for love, for domestic bliss. And as Edward became deeply attached to Kay, he tolerated with good grace her varieties of mood and inclination. Facilitating this was their close affinity in taste. They enjoyed reading poetry aloud to one another, for example – an outmoded entertainment today – and would recite *Kubla Khan*, or lines from Shakespeare, Byron, Keats, or Browning. Often Edward would sing in German, *'Du meine Seele, Du mein Schmerz'*, or mutter an equivalent in French as he buttoned up Kay's coat against the wind. They were a perfect complement to one another – he the modest, diffident observer as he strode along the pavement in his rounded artist's hat, she the ever-inspiring talking-companion who walked gaily by his side with firm brisk step.

And not without purpose. Together they arranged exhibitions of his work (discussed below) and otherwise enjoyed to the full a hectic cultural and social life. There were the Royal Academy soirées, the Aeolian Hall concerts given by the pianist Cortot, the Queen's Hall concerts of Myra Hess, and Baranova at Covent Garden. At the theatre they saw the leading actors and actresses of the time – John Gielgud as Romeo, Peggy Ashcroft as Tess in an adaptation of Hardy's novel, Eric Portman in a modern-dress version of *Julius Caesar*, along with Judith Anderson, Godfrey Tearle, and a host of others. They would dine at Odendino's or the Trocadero in evening attire ordered from the Galleries Lafayette. And, of course, in summer there was the tennis at Wimbledon.

They were also living above their means. The Wells trust executors could advance no money. And Edward was eventually obliged to sell his share in the valuable Church Row property in Hampstead to Edward Bridges Hardisty, his father's solicitor. Partly offsetting the drain on their resources, however, were the portrait commissions he was still receiving – from John Williams of Scorrier, for example, whose granddaughter, Daphne, he was invited to paint in late 1936. Such commissions enabled them to take more vacations – to the south-west of England, especially Devon, and later elsewhere, including Dent in Yorkshire.

It was in Devon, at the splendid family seat in Canonteign, that Edward Pownoll of the Pellew family (Lord Exmouth) and his wife resided, and there were invitations for Edward and Kay to visit them. Edward well remembered his portrait of Frances, Lady Exmouth, painted in about 1929; but this time he tackled a different, if not difficult subject – a stately, matriarchal cousin of the Pellew family named 'Aunt' Georgina C. Howard. The result was a splendid success. And the lady's proverbial grace and charm, conveyed somewhat in the style of a Thomas Lawrence painting, still resides on canvas at Canonteign for all to admire, a reminder that Edward's skill as a portraitist had in no way diminished by the later 1930s. 'We feel you have immortalized the dear old lady, surely unique in the world, in the most charming manner possible,' wrote Edward Pownoll; while Georgina herself echoed the sentiment with:

A line to tell you the picture arrived safe and sound this afternoon. It is in the Hall for the present and is much admired. . . . We must consult Edward P. where I shall hang. With love to Kathleen & self.

Yours affectionately,
G.C. Howard[4]

While in Devon, Edward and Kay took the opportunity to make a delightful trip to Teignmouth and Dawlish; and it was here by the seashore in 1937 that Edward painted his lyrical *Seagull*. It depicts a seagull circling low over a young woman reclining in the sand; Kay served as model. The whole setting, however, conveys mystery. The young woman reclines limply, a bit too limply, to the point where, instead of looking relaxed, she might become embedded in the sandy waves: whether she's dead or merely resting is left to the viewer's imagination. It is such fluidity in meaning that often makes Edward's work so intriguing.

His quality of deep sincerity, moreover, was brought out in the exhibitions he and Kay arranged of his drawings and watercolours – at Walker's Galleries in New Bond Street, for example, in June 1937 and November 1938. They received good reviews. In referring to the first one, *The Times*'s critic wrote that 'academic art can be done with taste or otherwise, and in the case of the exhibition of about 50 portraits and landscapes in oil and watercolour by E.F. Wells . . . the former is cordially recognised. Mr Wells is a thorough craftsman, and he never parades a skill that has not a serious intention.' While criticizing his *Repose* for having a discrepancy of tone in certain places because of the enormous difficulty the artist had set himself, the writer reserved much praise for individual portraits, among them that of Mrs Georgina Howard mentioned earlier. The *Morning Post*, in a review of the same month (June 1937), believed to have been written by Edward's friend Charles Marriott, stressed that the artist's portraits and landscapes 'appeal by their sincerity of purpose and careful craftsmanship'. While some papers, like the *Birmingham Post*, distributed praise fairly evenly among the major exhibits – including *Repose, The Boy and the Apple, The Chalk Pit*, and the portrait of Lady Romayne Cecil – other publications singled out *The Shower of Gold* for special praise. 'It is, with its glorious colour and its whole atmosphere, a joy,' enthused the critic of the *Hampstead and Highgate Express*. '*The Shower of Gold* is one of his RA exhibits,' echoed 'K.B.' in *Walker's Monthly*, 'Both these reproductions [the other being *The Boy and the Apple*] are typical examples of his work, and clearly show not only the influence and subtlety, but the secret of the Old Masters.' Another critic, writing in the November 1938 issue of this same periodical, saw in Edward's second exhibition at Walker's Galleries, which comprised his Italian scenes, evidence of a master draughtsman (as he was later to prove himself in his oil paintings), while also commenting on the influence of Turner and Ruskin on his work. The review was signed 'K.S.D.' and a pen-and-ink and wash reproduction of Edward's *Viterbo* was printed alongside. A further critic, 'M.M.', preferred his Italian watercolours to his drawings. In emphasizing that Edward above all painted what he saw, the reviewer felt that his use of colour enabled him to change his vision completely and to obtain a tremendous fluency of expression. 'Forms and shadows resolve themselves gracefully into attractive designs; small, perhaps troublesome details merge themselves unostentatiously into the whole; and the general efffect is one of lively and interesting painting.'[5]

These exhibitions were not, however, very successful financially. Granted that the first one at least was partly a loan exhibition, Augustus Walker, an old friend of Edward and owner-director of Walker's Galleries, perhaps put it succinctly when he told Edward that he considered him a first-class artist, 'if only you would choose topics that people liked'. Despite these half-successes, or half-failures, in which Edward's refusal to resort to a publicity agent was doubtless a factor, he would never utter a word of reproach. With his quiet strength he took everything in his stride, even when inwardly aroused. On the credit side, successful exhibitions were given privately in their own home. Indeed, people would often come and ask how to organize exhibitions themselves.

Here, often in relaxed hours with friends, they might play cards or parlour games such as mah-jong or 'Lexicon'. Or Willy Turner might converse with Edward about some exciting find he had come across on his travels in the art world. Sooner or later, however, they would entertain on a lavish scale. There were the cocktail parties, dinners for local celebrities, champagne suppers by candlelight laid out on their Jacobean refectory table. And New Year's Eve at 39 Parkhill Road always resounded to the tune of 'Auld Lang Syne'.

Sometimes a violin performance might be given, an accompanyist playing on their solid Hagspiel grand. This piano had fitted easily into their 10 ft high drawing room both spatially and acoustically, the room filling with its deeply resonant notes. And Kay herself would play for hours the sonatas of Beethoven, along with pieces by Chopin and Grieg, as well as much modern music. Edward would listen approvingly, as he glanced over his newspaper in between the fortissimos, stoically attuning himself to Scriabin or Delius because he knew her tastes were more Romantic and modern than his own. His favourite wireless programmes were the Promenade Concerts conducted by Sir Henry Wood, broadcast over the BBC National Service. To the music of Bach or Handel, Edward would listen with rapt attention, tapping out the rhythm with his foot. He loved classical music. To the three big 'Bs' (Bach, Beethoven and Brahms) could be added his preference for the two big 'Hs' (Handel and Haydn), the two big 'Ms' (Mozart and Mendelssohn), and the two big 'Ss' (Schubert and Schumann). Indeed, with his wife's fine playing close at hand, he could find in music an inspiration for his art.

The fabulous parties they gave, meanwhile, drew a growing circle of professionals. There was Jim Byam Shaw, the art critic, for example, and Frank Bennett, the period painter – an old friend of Edward, as we have seen, who had married the beautiful Margaret Pellew. (A great admirer of Edward's work, Margaret was to be tragically and fatally injured later in a fire accident in her home). And there was Bill Wells himself, a leading light at any party, who, after a stint at such institutes as Courtauld's and the Warburg, was to distinguish himself later in the world of curatorship. On Kay's side of the family, there was Aileen Hardinge Jarvis, her sister from America, who had been aide to Ely Culbertson in devising the rules for contract bridge. Edward's painting of her before her return on the Cunard luxury liner, the *Queen Mary* was greeted with much acclaim.

It was a circle of more than just dilettantes and dabblers who surrounded Edward and Kay; but, for those who did, it was still an age of innocence, in which arts of all kinds were discussed intelligently, though generally divorced from the harsh realities of social issues, war, or revolution. Here was the last sputtering of an age reflecting the past, rounding out the era of the late King George V, and signalling the last triumphs of courtesy – as well as class distinction – before what remained of the old Europe was to crumble forever.

Edward and Kay continued to live calmly in this atmosphere. Giving little thought to change, they lived it up to the hilt, with Edward overlooking whatever faults he thought his wife possessed because he appreciated her personal interest in his work. They were true partners. From tennis to ballroom-dancing (in which he now took lessons at Madame Vandyck's and whose director, Madelaine Vandyck, had sat to him), they were always together, sharing common interests, planning new ideas. But all this activity was beginning to tax Edward's strength. Moreover his deafness in one ear did not improve; it was believed to have been caused by damage to the Eustacian tube some years previously.

Aged sixty-three in 1939, he had now reached a stage in life when he needed to reflect. When left to himself his routine habits claimed him. On completing any task to his satisfaction he would often whistle through his teeth as if expressing to the world that he was happy. He might whistle with delight, for example, at the finishing touches of a brushstroke on a canvas; another delight was to solve part of a crossword puzzle, eyes darting, fingers drumming on the arm-rest for more right answers. He was good at puzzles, especially difficult ones, the squares in *The Times* or *Daily Telegraph* rapidly filling with his pencilled letters. In other respects, he would mull over thoughts in his mind long before he expressed them, till they were uttered with the exactitude of a considered statement, in the manner of a Victorian. They were the words of one who reflected without being pedantic, who opined without being opinionated; and he was rarely contentious.

His thoughts were largely concerned with art or literature, with the pleasures of day-to-day existence or the wisdom of past ages, but rarely of the future. It was as if he had earned his happiness and was now enjoying it to the full – the glow of contentment blinding him, as with so many others, to menacing clouds ahead.

CHAPTER SEVEN

THE SECOND WORLD WAR AND TRIUMPH

The bombs started to fall early in September 1940. France had fallen; now it was England's turn to suffer. Prime Minister Chamberlain, who had failed dismally to come to terms with Hitler, had resigned and been replaced by a defiant Churchill. The *Luftwaffe* was instructed to bomb London. And the house on Parkhill Road took in the cacophony of anti-aircraft gunfire from Hampstead Heath and Primrose Hill, and from the mobile ack-ack guns along the streets. Louder came the whistling explosives in reply, and later, the sucking sound of the land mines. Above the barrage balloons, away from the searchlights, the *Luftwaffe* bombers – Dorniers and Heinkels among them – discharged their loads with deadly effect, but haphazardly, as if in a hurry to get back home. Were there enough Messerschmitt 109Es, the pilots might have wondered, to give them fighter protection against the deadly Spitfires? But such questions did not concern the household on Parkhill Road. The mood was numbness, going through the motions of living – fear without much time for prayer. 'No herald angels or German bombers broke through the canopy of fog that hid the sky,' as one friend stoically wrote to them on a merciful night in that mad season of autumn 1940 during the blitz on London.

But most of the time, the plaintive wail of the air-raid warnings, the thud of falling masonry, the clang of ambulances charging toward the fires and wreckage, were all part of human existence. London glowed like a pagan ritual out of a Wagner opera. And when the 'all clears' came from the sirens, giving a brief respite in the routine struggle for survival, the blazing fires continued as if barely touched by the hoses.

Despite the horror of it all, few had thought the worst could really happen here, here in one's very home. To ease the tension during the lulls, the Wells household passed the time calmly playing cards or chess. The common peril drew everyone closer – there was Kay's son, their dedicated maid Olive and her husband, and the rest of their staff, to complete the picture. The faces all looked grey-blue, expressionless, in the half-light of the blackout. This is what air raids did to you.

Then came the hit. It missed the house by inches; the bomb landed right outside their front gate. But it was a delayed-action bomb – a miracle, in fact, since this meant that all the household members were saved, along with the house itself, and all its contents, including Edward's paintings. But 39 Parkhill Road would never be the same again. Wardens sealed off the street and told all residents to evacuate immediately. In the commotion Olive, together with her husband, simply vanished into the night and Edward and Kay never saw them again. A few days later Kay's son crept back into the house, past that terrifying hole made by the unexploded bomb, to retrieve a few things for Edward and to stack up his paintings. To leave them on the wall would have invited disaster. He took the canvasses down, and stored and shielded them as best as he could without the availability of sandbags, in the course of which *The Shower of Gold* received a slight tear in the right foreground. But the paintings were safer than they had been; and by an act of fate they survived the devastation.

Virtually bombed out of their home, the family took refuge in a nearby hotel in Belsize Park. Called the Ormonde Hotel, it contained a motley collection of nerve-racked civilians, war personnel, Jewish refugees, bombed-out clerics and plain eccentrics. 'I'm the Vicar of Hampstead,' one tattered new arrival announced to the lady hotel-keeper, a Mrs Lawless, the worthy padre's coat and trousers covered with white plaster from his demolished home. 'Never mind. Come in,' Mrs Lawless replied with quick riposte. Everyone's spirits were brave, able to make light of tragedy; and this included Edward and Kay. The latter, incidentally, was unable to do war-work because she had to look after Edward, who since June 1940 had been convalescing from a stroke – a serious, near fatal illness in which he had lost the use of a leg. But Edward never once complained. (Curiously, his disability hardly affected his art in the long run.) Compounding his misfortune, of course, was the fact that professionally there was little doing in the world of portraiture for the duration.

Nevertheless, Edward still managed to paint a few interesting portraits during the war years, including two of Kay's son. A forceful half-face completed at their home in 1940 combines the dreaminess of youth with the confusions of adolescence – about right and wrong, survival and death – which everyone was subjected to at this time. A second portrait, also done at their home, shows him in a reflective and maturer mood when he was up at Oxford two years later. It is likewise half-face, but with a fuller figure, replete with college blazer, the whole poise bent on study, the war temporarily forgotten. A most interesting portrait outside the family circle was that of Marlys Ludicke, a girl of nine portrayed in ballet costume, painted in about 1942. Edward had already made a drawing of her, which had prompted her father, Harold Ludicke, to write: 'We do not know how to thank you enough for the lovely picture you drew of Marlys. It is splendid. We feel very flattered about it and of course very proud. It came as a great surprise.'[1] Kay in particular had long had close relations with the Ludicke family, who, it will be recalled, gave her hospitality as a teenager after her mother's death. Indeed Harold's sister, Dorothy, became one of Kay's closest friends. It was not surprising therefore that Edward executed a number of works for this family. As well as a portrait of Dorothy herself done in 1937, and a drawing from a photograph of her deceased brother Bill, Edward had also painted Harold's wife Charlotte, thus anticipating the Marlys portrait mentioned above. Concluding this group of wartime paintings is a small panel in colour of Louise Ludicke (Harold's and Dorothy's mother), done posthumously from a snapshot. With his uncanny gift of re-creating personality, he captures poignantly her gently laughing face with its expressive humour in a way that this same photograph, perhaps, could never equal.

Regarding exhibitions, the one at the Brook Street Art Gallery in November 1939, that at Heffer's of Cambridge in May 1942 ('There is a luminosity which characterises all his work, and an avoidance of that excess of white which is so often a feature of contemporary paintings,' enthused one reviewer initialled 'R.H.'), and the one at Frost and Reed's Clare Street Art Gallery in Bristol two years later were not very profitable, though Edward and Kay can be forgiven for having tried. A gleam of success in this wartime gloom, however, was the acceptance by the Royal Academy of his *Spring Woodland* watercolour for the season of 1941. This was Edward's last painting to be exhibited at this institution.

At the height of the bombing, meanwhile, when Edward and Kay were staying at the Ormonde Hotel, it was welcome news when the Gurneys (of the banking family) invited them both in October 1940 for a brief visit to their home in Walsingham Abbey. Lady Agatha suggested that the famous mill at Cley-Next-Sea in Norfolk might be convenient for them to stay in as it was vacant, and so there they went by the end of October.

The round rooms with the huge stationary mill-wheel peeping in, as it were, like a permanent stare from the past, gave them a curious but relaxed sensation. As proof of their comfort they stayed here the best part of a year. The snow decked everything with a thick blanket of white that winter. When it melted and the outline of the landscape sank back toward the coastal horizon, splendid views were offered from every angle. There were moments of excitement too, such as greeting Gerald Ackermann, the watercolourist whom Edward had known for many years, not to mention the news of the Royal Academy acceptance mentioned above. But Edward found little inspiration to paint. The misty, furrowed salt-marshes, flecked with crying seagulls and herons, darting among the hues of pink and brown turning to sepia (which might normally have inspired him) barely concealed the terror of hidden mines, including the spot where Admiral Lord North was killed. No one could really escape the war, nor make lyricism out of it. Hitler invaded Russia in the summer; and Edward and Kay listened on the wireless with rapt attention and not a little amusement to the rhetoric of Lord Haw-Haw (William Joyce, who had replaced Bailey Stuart in this role). Indeed, as the months of 1941 dragged on, the late summer mists became increasingly gloomy. The enemy, it seemed, were winning the war.

It was good to get back to their home in Hampstead that autumn and let in a little fresh air to the house that had been spared. The UXB, or unexploded bomb, had long been dismantled and removed by those brave bomb-disposal men of the Royal Engineers, and 39 Parkhill Road stood there just as before, though now it was surrounded by gaping ruins. A whole convent of nuns had been wiped out in the next street. Everywhere there were visible signs of deadly war, but lightening the gloom was the fact that the air raids came less often. At least the Battle of Britain was over; now Edward and Kay could pick up the threads of their lives again like the seasoned Londoners they had become.

Curiously, it was a Japanese, before his country came into the war, who inspired Edward's next portrait. It was of Mr Toshio Urabe, a retired diplomat posted at the time to the Japanese embassy in London and who was staying as a guest in their home. He was a knowledgeable man, and imparted a warm friendliness. Neither sitter nor artist allowed the deteriorating relations between their two countries to interfere with professional courtesy, which they maintained throughout. Mr Urabe was genuinely appreciative of all things English, while Edward with his usual tact was quick to point out that Japan had been England's ally in the previous war. An amusing incident once affected Edward, Kay and Mr Urabe. One night as they were playing bridge a smiling policeman called and cautioned them to fix their black-out properly.

'What a bother,' said Kay nonchalantly after inviting him in, 'Let's leave it for a while.'

'Madam, if you don't fix it this minute, there will be a bother,' replied the smiling policeman, only with a different kind of smile. The black-out was fixed. On the other side of the world Pearl Harbor was bombed soon after this incident took place, on 7 December 1941, and Mr Urabe was interned. But not before Edward had, with great depth of concentration, swiftly completed a portrait with which the sitter was delighted. Nearly fifty years later, in 1989, Mr Urabe wrote that, though his portrait had received a slight scratch, it was in good condition, hanging on the wall of his study. He remembered having hesitated about having it done at the time, and that it was Kay who had finally persuaded him to proceed with it. He was indeed very happy to have the portrait and to have made the decision that he did.[2] It is now in his home at Setagaya-Ku, Tokyo. As mentioned previously, Mr Urabe also possesses a portrait of the artist's mother, which he purchased in 1988.

Apart from small canvasses, Edward continued to rest during the following months. It was a rest disturbed by the sad news of his sister's death (and that of her husband Jack at about the same time), which also entailed the selling of some assets of their joint Wells trust to help pay the death duties. Shrinking incomes affected everyone. For those like the Wells family the aim was to survive as gracefully as possible, with rations getting tighter and with Lord Woolton the food minister assuring everyone that there would always be enough potatoes to survive on. Despite the U-boat war which was severely damaging Britain's lifeline, however, the real good news was America's entry into the war. Already in 1942 she was marshalling her vast resources to back up the Allied side.

A refreshing interlude where Edward and Kay were concerned was the invitation they received in September of this year, 1942, to visit Pownoll Pellew (son of Edward and Frances) and his glamorous Spanish wife, María Luisa (Marquesa de Olias, of the Urquijo banking family). These two lived modestly at Lustleigh, the family seat of the Viscount Exmouths at Canonteign having been lent for the duration as a hostel for infants. Pownoll and María wanted a painting of their little daughter, Mary Rose, a beautiful child of about five years old. Edward's portrait of her is of great sensitivity, and now hangs in María Luisa's splendid dower house at Canonteign. Pownoll observed that Mary Rose in some ways looked like her beautiful grandmother, Frances.[3]

Back home in London, while Kay's son was departing for war service in the spring of 1943, Edward could sit back with some consolation that the war was getting on, the tide turning in the Allies' favour. In Tunis, as at Stalingrad – 'Tunisgrad', commentators dubbed it – the enemy had suffered catastrophic defeats. There was a cartoon in the paper showing Hitler asking Napoleon what he did about Russia; 'I *did*,' answered Napoleon flatly. Edward guffawed at the caption.

During the next months they received good news about Edward's son, Bill. While attached to the field security wing of the Intelligence Corps he had became attached to a lovely dancer named Catharine Marks. He had first met her at 39 Parkhill Road through Kay's own fortuitous introduction. The result was not only a successful marriage, but an equally successful portrait of the bride by Edward. Catharine had joined ENSA (an agency for entertaining the troops), and the couple found themselves in Cairo that Christmas of 1943, an ideal place for both their wedding and honeymoon. They were to pursue distinguished careers after the war – Bill as curator of the renowned Burrell Collection in Glasgow, Catharine as founder, teacher and director of a flourishing school of dancing in the same city. Her portrait currently hangs in their home at Islip, near Oxford. That of her handsome brother Michael Marks, an RAF pilot, hangs near it – an equally attractive portrait Edward made posthumously from a photograph, Michael having been tragically shot down over the Rhine.

Despite the rising optimism about the war's progress, Edward and Kay still felt in pretty low water – exhibitions were 'out', portrait commissions few. Indeed Christmas in 1943 was the last one they ever fully spent at 39 Parkhill Road, for the struggle of running a home was becoming too much for them. So next year they finally moved to a guest-house at Crowhurst Park in Sussex. It was situated near Battle, close by the site where the historic Battle of Hastings had once been fought. D-Day had come at last; and as Allied soldiers blooded their way across Normandy, it seemed to Edward and the other guests that this was like a Norman Conquest in reverse.

Set on a height in a sweep of beautiful valley, Crowhurst offered an inspiring vantage point, and Edward did some interesting work here. In a fit of playfulness he touched off a sketch of a baby while the mother wasn't looking – the beautiful mother being Lorna Byrne, sister, incidentally, of Lord Peter Henderson, who became Keeper of the House of Lords. It is a pencil drawing of a sleeping *Jane Byrne*, whom Edward caught as he looked down over her cradle. She had gone to sleep sucking her thumb, but at this point her mouth had opened, thumb abandoned, and her cap having slipped gave her the look of a Tudor infant. Other works painted at Crowhurst included fine portraits of Mrs R.M. Tull and Miss Mona Larmer, both fellow guests; while another was a sky scene with a flying bomb racing across it.

In respect of the last work, this was the time of the famous V1 and V2 rockets. As Edward was wrestling with an oil landscape on the Downs, a V1 pilotless plane (dubbed a or 'buzz bomb' or 'doodle-bug') sped across the sky. Undisturbed by its lethal destination, he calmly painted it in – a fitting tribute to satanic power and the inanity of war. Sold by Southeby's at their south Kensington branch many years later in about 1960, it is now believed to be located in an RAF facility, though its exact whereabouts is unknown. Kay herself, incidentally, experienced the effects of the more terrible V2 rocket which came after the buzz bomb. She was phoning Edward from London when her hair suddenly seemed to stand on end, dress billowing in a rush of air just before an appalling, almost instantaneous detonation. With the impact presumed to have been but half a mile away and with the effect on her being so cataclysmic at this distance, Kay reasoned that anyone much nearer would have had little chance of surviving. Despite all this, and because there was little you could do with no advance warning, everyone had grown hardened to thoughts of danger. Indeed, governments on both sides in the war were learning that air raids only stiffen people's morale.

Sadly, their dog, 'Tigger', a feisty wire-haired terrier, had to be put in kennels somewhere on the Downs because they now had to go to the West Country on an assignment. Edward had been fond of Tigger, perhaps seeing in him shades of his other dog, 'Ponto', from Beulah Hill days. But Tigger's fate was mild compared with that of pet dogs in Nazi Germany ordered to be destroyed so as to save food – a fate that offered meager consolation to pet lovers on both sides of the Channel.

The assignment mentioned above was a commission from G.P. Williams Esq. of Four Burrow House, Scorrier, Cornwall, who wanted Edward to paint his father-in-law, who lived in the west of England. The Williams family were Edward's friends of long standing, as seen in previous contexts; and Mr Williams was frank enough to make it clear that he wanted the painting strictly for his wife, and not for the father-in-law![4] Presumably Edward was entrusted to give the message.

Despite the odd commission here and there, Edward and Kay by this time had to think out what to do to keep themselves afloat. An exhibition in Bristol had only had limited success, so the idea came to them to open an art gallery of their own. The time to do it was now, they both agreed, while rents were still low in wartime. Accordingly, on returning to London later in 1944, they sold the balance of their lease on 39 Parkhill Road – the solid structure of their home that had withstood so much and sheltered them for so long, was now finally abandoned – and eventually after much searching they rented an ideal

The Buzz Bomb Over the Downs

gallery. It was located at the corner of Sloane Street and Cadogan Place in the Hans Town (Knightsbridge) part of London. It was a master-stroke on Kay's part, whose find it was, giving them a welcome uplift after so much adversity and upheaval.

At first they had thought of renting an enormous studio, encouraging clientele to visit through extensive advertising. Accordingly they inspected the house of the eighteenth-century artist, George Romney, on Holly Hill in Hampstead, which was available. The huge rabbit-warrened structure, dubbed 'Romney's Folly' on this account (perhaps appropriately in view of this artist's infatuation with Lady Hamilton), was none the less saved from the misnomer by its truly palatial studio with handsome stone fireplaces once giving on to piles of antique casts which Romney's friend Flaxman had gathered for him in Italy. At first glance the house seemed ideal for Edward and Kay, but an eerie experience on one visit, apparently involving shades of Romney himself, not to mention pungent smells of earth in unlikely places was enough to put both of them off then and there, and they promptly left the premises as fast as they could, abandoning any attempt to secure a lease!

Having given up the idea of a lofty studio, they eventually found the more business-like premises already referred to – at 162 Sloane Street. It had probably once been a drawing room of the Georgian house ending on Cadogan Place and had subsequently been turned into a fashion shop. It was perfect for an art gallery, being lined with oak panelling, well lit, and in a good location. Moreover, despite the risks involved and their own lack of experience in a venture of this sort, Kay successfully urged that the gallery be confined to showing only Edward's work.

It was opened in February 1945, with the last bombs still falling. And in spite of discouraging opinions – 'Fancy opening a gallery with the war on'; 'You can't run a gallery on one man's work' – it survived four years and was a great success. This was an exciting time for Edward; and to be nearer to the action they moved into a flat at the end of Cadogan Place conveniently adjoining the premises. By 1990, incidentally, this little flat at No. 88, along with the gallery itself, has been absorbed by a renovation project so huge that these corner premises today are no longer recognizable.

Less than three months after the gallery was opened peace came at last with VE day. Their enterprise was well timed, and Edward received a dazzling array of portrait commissions. A special demand was for reproductions from photographs, especially of relatives lost in the war.[5] Indeed, this facet of the enterprise earned almost as much revenue as the sale of the work itself. The fact was that Edward, as we have seen, had an uncanny knack of reading a photographic image and transposing the likeness and basic characteristics on to canvas without ever having known the person concerned. A compassionate man, he knew how to convey comfort to the sad-hearted.

All this, however, was beginning to tax his strength. He was now nearly seventy; and though Kay had always been there to nurse him to full recovery since his illness, the question was raised as to how long he could keep up this heavy pace without a relapse. For the time being, however, he successfully concealed his growing tiredness in face of so many engagements, thus relieving his wife of some anxiety. Partly prompting this was the buoyant fact that the gallery itself was doing well.

The first painting ever sold there was an oil, *Man on a White Horse*, which went to a Mrs Ewing. Another, *The Boy and the Peaches*, was nearly snapped up by a passing motorist before it finally went to Mona Larmer – the same whom Edward had recently painted; while *Nan Combing Her Hair* went to Mrs Cedarwell Browne, whom Edward was to paint as a gallery portrait, and the *Three Roses* went to a lady from Scandinavia. Watercolours sold rapidly, titles and purchasers comprising a list simply too long to enumerate. It gave Edward and Kay immense satisfaction to have someone come in and say, 'I should like that picture!' And the subjects chosen ranged widely, from domestic scenes to still life and scenes from nature. Humanity was again seeking humanity, and nature, after the inhuman horrors of war.

As for portrait commissions, of both 'live' and photographic subjects, these became so frequent that Edward was now working virtually from canvas to canvas. Actual sitters during the gallery's lifetime included: the four sons of Mrs Mabel Delaforce; Lady Norton Griffiths; Miss Haviland; Francis Hughes; Mrs Rose Leigh; Major E.G. Pratt; members of the Pretzlick family (Charles senior and his two daughters, Mrs Elfreda Bearman and Tilla, Viscountess Scarsdale); Victor and Pamela Riddle; Mrs Victor Savitt; and the Hon. Jane Walsh, daughter of Anne Walsh. A sample of the pleasure given to these sitters and their families is summed up in the comment by the last-named: 'The picture arrived safely this morning and is already hung in the drawing-room with the other portraits. It is charming and we are all quite delighted with it. . . . We are also very pleased with the frame.'[6]

Other portraits were painted in the war years independently of the gallery. These included one of Marguerite Beauvais, pianist and magnificent exponent of Schumann, and another of Mrs Laura Mengel-Byrne; no doubt the records of other sitters as yet unidentified will eventually come to light.

There were, of course, the inevitable disappointments. One day a man came into the gallery, and, having admired Edward's work, told him excitedly that he could produce a most attractive sitter for him. Terms for the portrait were discussed, and the sitter was none other than the man's wife – an ethereal beauty indeed – calm, lyrical, like a Botticelli. Her husband was very keen on the project, affirming that Edward alone was the artist most fit to paint her. But the sittings proved rather an anti-climax. The beautiful wife continually dissolved into tears, and Edward was hard put to cope with this phenomenon. As Kay took her for a walk in Cadogan Gardens to find out the problem, the lady declared that she and Edward had met in a previous life, 'flying through the ether together, holding hands,' as she roundly described it. This realization, she claimed, was what made her cry uncontrollably. Upon returning to the gallery they did their best to calm her, but the resumed portrait was not a great success. Edward behaved with commendable composure in the face of so tense an encounter; but the result was, to say the least, not at all like the serene Botticelli he had at first envisaged! Was the man to be pitied, or should it be the poor wife? Edward and Kay never did find the key to this puzzle.

Several other anecdotes could have been told about their patrons were it not for the confidentiality they owed them. When the gallery finally closed in 1949, it was like a curtain coming down on so many old acquaintances who had helped the gallery achieve so much. This marked the end of a late but successful phase in Edward's life. Able at last to escape the constant demand for portrait work, he could rest for a whole year in the privacy of their cosy flat at 88 Cadogan Place. Serenity prevailed. But even here the urge to paint returned, and Edward even thought of approaching the Fine Art Society in Bond Street to canvas for commissions. He and Kay may have looked inwards, reminiscing and congratulating, but with gritty determination they were planning to scale yet higher peaks – with Kay by now the stronger force in their relationship.

In other respects they enjoyed simple pleasures – visits by friends, or a private viewing of the artist's work. In moments of relaxation they would mull over the Lord Peter Wimsey stories (Dorothy Sayers could still hold her own against Agatha Christie), Arnold Bennett's books, Dickens's *Bleak House*. Edward also liked spy stories, including any that harked back to the First World War, and, of course, there were always crosswords. Listening to the wireless during the war, he had guffawed at the buffoonery of Tommy Handley and his gang, though by this time it was the Brains Trust that had come to the fore; and he loved Gilbert and Sullivan. Their outings had included the occasional concert, visits to Southeby's or Christie's, visits to Harrods, but they rarely went out now, not even to shows or cinemas as had been their custom. Kay, however, would take him into Hyde Park or Kensington, where they watched the riders go by on Rotten Row, the Serpentine in the distance making a picture all of its own. Here they might picnic together, communing or just basking in solitude. It was a carefree year for them in 1949, spun out on the expanse of open grass, on a park bench, beneath the time-worn trees. Much of England agreed with them, as the nation too was in a kind of tranquil glow, basking in past glory, struggling to recover, too poor for luxurious living. Indeed the state of emergency that had long been decreed was still in force. As everywhere in Europe, it was a time for reflection, a time for reconstruction.

With the ending of the Second World War, Edward's second baptism of fire was over. He was enjoying its rewards – though still with the dignity of the pre-1914 generation (and in the old-fashioned manner, incidentally, of still clinging to his 'cut-throat' blade when shaving). Edward, however, was not an archaic bore. He welcomed technical innovation in many respects, and showed a great interest in the novel idea of long-playing records. He was open-minded about many things (unless it be trade union management, which made his lips curl), and he had not the slightest animosity toward any social or ethnic group – except, of course, toward murderers. Spicing the news at the time was the sensational Haig case that told of the macabre horrors of this famous criminal who had the habit of drowning his victims in drums of corrosive acid. Perversely perhaps, such chilling oddities took everyone's mind off the grim task, the drab routine of daily living after the war.

Edward and Kay, though, now had some glamour in their own lives of which to be proud. They certainly had both guts and inner resources, and these were soon to be put to the test in yet another enterprise. Though there had been personal tragedy in his first marriage, and also in his second marriage in terms of his grave illness and the Second World War itself, Edward with his persistent work and unyielding purpose had weathered all the storms. It was only a pity that his professional success came just too late for him to reap the fullest advantage. But this success, at the end of a long ordeal, stretching back to the darkest days of 1940, had sharpened his perception, inwardly, secretly, down to the last canvas he ever touched.

One gallery portrait deserves mentioning here as a wonderful surprise in Edward's late career – the head-and-shoulders portrait of Mrs Doris Bowyer. Adorning today the Maurice Bowyer home near Sherborne, Dorset, the half-figure stands out markedly, looking as fresh and alive as when the sitter first faced the artist in 1947. With bright blue eyes in rounded face, her bright blonde hair set against a sweep of lighter background, the young lady presents a gift of consummate beauty to all who view her – warm, ethereal, the essence of serenity on canvas. Indeed the portrait would make any room a place of joy and happiness: proof that Edward as a man over seventy was as skilled and vibrant in saluting youth as when he was a younger man himself. Maurice Bowyer, incidentally, became an avid collector of E.F. Wells's watercolours, and featuring among them is *The Blackmoor Vale*, which graces the same house.

CHAPTER EIGHT

THE WATCH THAT DIDN'T STOP

A record of the final phase of Edward's life would be incomplete without a summary of his opinions about other artists. Kay had taken note of them over the years. Now, at mid-century, during the quiet times they spent in Hyde Park, she questioned him further, and the substance of his comments is given here in more or less their original order.[1]

Edward considered Rembrandt about the greatest painter of them all. This stemmed from his imagination, from his supreme technical skill. And Jan Steen, among other Dutch artists, came close behind. Sir Joshua Reynolds, by contrast, had less imagination and originality; but he did study the 'Venetian secret' (on which Edward set great store), and got into much trouble for keeping it to himself. Reynolds skirted this subject, for example, in his presentation speeches to students of the Royal Academy; and on other issues was envied by Gainsborough. But Reynolds was good in his treatment of light and shade, and in quality and effect could bear some comparison with Rembrandt and Titian. Considering his output of one portrait a week, moreover, his performance was amazing. As to Gainsborough, Edward had a high regard for his sensitivity and pure artistry, with his deft hand and flowing brushwork like handwriting. Indeed he gave him higher marks than Reynolds. But it was Titian whom Edward deemed the greatest colourist of all time (which made him virtually share the first place with Rembrandt). Titian's 'Venetian secret', however, with its measurement by the eye enabling the painter to imitate the true tones and values of nature, was in all probability derived from Giorgione. In other respects Titian's work had dignity, harmony, grandeur of design, and perfect imitation of natural effect.

Continuing his comments on the British school of artists, Edward recounted an amusing story told by Charles Lutyens concerning the famous Scottish painter Sir Henry Raeburn when he was a young man. Desiring technical advice, Raeburn went to see the elderly Reynolds, who gave Raeburn the usual advice to 'go to Italy and study the Old Masters'; but thinking Raeburn rather likeable despite his pushy persistence, Reynolds offered to show the young man how to do it, 'if you would stay on your side of the border, and not interfere with me in the south!' A veiled compliment indeed, seeing that the young Scot in the end fully justified the senior man's hunch about his ability. Edward, incidentally, was angry with the artist and critic, Clive Bell, who wrote an article claiming that Raeburn was 'meretricious'. Edward regarded this charge as ridiculous. Raeburn's characterization was superb in his view, unlike the uneven Romney's, with knowledge so much at his fingertips that he could put it down with an easy sincerity, if at times slickly.

Regarding the British school of landscape, if Constable in Edward's opinion scored as high as the young Gainsborough, Turner scored even higher. He was arguably the greatest British painter. He was a genius, an extremely hard worker, a true poet in feeling and technique – in his paintings the trees were gorgeous, the effects of sun and mist powerful and imaginative. Pleasing to Edward was Turner's total absorption of the strength and beauty of nature. Some of his later, big pictures may have been cheapened by the influence of drinking too much sherry(!), but his smaller landscapes were as perfect as they could be. Of Thomas Girtin, who worked with Turner in early days, Edward noted Turner's comment that 'had Girtin lived, I would never have been'.

As to the Pre-Raphaelites and Burne-Jones, as well as Watts, Edward held all of these in less esteem than Turner. He liked Whistler and Walter Sickert, and admired even more John Sargent at the Slade ('By Jove, he's nearly got it!'). On the other hand, Edward was more critical of the Impressionist-style work of Philip Wilson Steer, whom he also knew ('There are clever draughtsmen like him about, good at putting on paint, but the effect of their colouring is so bad'). Regarding Augustus John, Edward was ambivalent. He viewed him as a cross between a pseudo Old Master, imitating El Greco to the point of pastiche, and a most original worker, especially with the small panels of women done in his youth. He was plainly silly at times, yet he could be decorative and challenging; often inaccurate, yet he could be a good draughtsman; slick, but giving great impressions of power with his lines. Edward was less charitable to Reggie Eves. Undeniably charming and good-looking, Eves in Edward's view lacked sound knowledge and on this account surely did deserve the charge of being 'meretricious'. He may have been good at characterization, but he did it in a slapdash manner for cheap effect. Edward well remembered how Eves's work was dubbed 'Eves's flicks' at the Slade! Many of the above he also knew at the Chelsea Arts Club.

As for the so-called London Group, he gave them the lowest marks of all, castigating them for lack of study, academic unsoundness, and sheer inability to draw. Edward admired the French school, however, especially the Impressionists. They broke away from stiff classical traditions, and attempted to express outdoor effects of nature, even if they did exaggerate colour to emphasize their observation. Monet, Cézanne, and others created innovation and laughed at the standards of the Paris Salon. They were wholesome and sincere, in no way charlatans, who broke away from tight drawing in an attempt to paint *plein air*. They were nearly all of them great artists (with Renoir, perhaps, a little less great than the others).

Of the Spanish school, Edward said little, being generally rather non-committal in this field. Velázquez in his view lacked the luminosity of Titian, though he liked his silvery scheme of colour. As a court painter, Velázquez gave a good rendering of character, while Murillo at the opposite extreme was best at the daily lives of beggars and ordinary street people – better, even, than with his religious pictures, that were 'not of the highest order' compared with Italian counterparts. With regard to Goya, the young Picasso and Dali, these giants of creativity apparently escaped his recorded comment altogether.

Conservative as Edward may have been in his judgements, in contrast to the more 'modern' perspective of much twentieth-century art, the type of imaginative traditional realism which he propounded still holds its own today. Thus Edward's work finds its place in the commercial art market and in the hands of private connoisseurs. Indeed, having found a certain level, it may permanently ride out the trends and counter-trends of the years to come.

In the mid-twentieth century however, Edward and Kay were less concerned with posterity than with the need to survive after the considerable loss of revenue from giving up their art gallery. The time for rest and reflection was over. They had to leave the Elysian Fields and think about their finances all over again. The cost of living was rising ever higher with inflation, and their private income barely stretched. Kay thought that the best move now would be to exhibit the still considerable number of E.F. Wells watercolours for sale to the public, without incurring the exacting task of portrait commissions. Edward was now in his mid-seventies, and this type of work was taxing his strength. Indeed, this has been the main reason why the gallery had had to be given up in the first place. Picture cleaning was one occupation of moderate exertion for both of them, and an encouraging letter in this respect came from their old solicitor, A.F. Lindner of Hardisty and Lindner: 'I cannot tell you how pleased I was,' he wrote, in referring to a portrait of his partner done many years previously, which Edward had cleaned and touched up, 'to see the picture of Edward Hardisty. You really have made the picture live and it now is a great credit to you as an artist.'[2] This kind of work, however, brought modest rewards compared with the sale of Edward's watercolours, which was to prove a grand finale to his artistic career.

By this time they were becoming past masters at giving exhibitions, having learned the ropes through hard experience. Bond Street was to be avoided. The galleries there were usually booked up for months in advance and were very expensive. So, after making a thorough analysis of their needs and problems, they searched for something nearer their home ground in Sloane Street. They knew exactly what they were looking for; the question was whether they would find it.

One of the first essentials in an exhibition, they had learnt, was daylight –

the stronger, the better. Artificial light in a room destroyed blues and distorted other colours. A second factor was accessibility. It was no use having perfect conditions in a room if people had to make an effort to get there. Reaching the top of a building, climbing long stairs, or even using a lift could deter a potential viewer. Another essential was having the proper size of room. It would not have to be too large, because this would require the expense of too many frames. A suitable number of watercolours for a one-man show was twenty-four, with replacements at hand; and they needed to be all in one row. A double line of pictures, they had learnt, was tiring on the eyes since the average person could not concentrate for long in viewing and easily became confused. As for the frames themselves, these had to be perfect – no shabby, makeshift *passe-partout*. And catalogues were definitely 'out'; they had abandoned these long ago. This was because viewers found them a nuisance as they fumbled with spectacles, handbags, or umbrellas, often dropping them in the process. Much better was a small card tucked into the lower corner of each frame, giving the title or location of the subject, along with the artist's name and price. These were all the essential details viewers really wanted to know. Edward and Kay also abandoned the idea of having a private viewing. They had found from experience that people would stand about gossiping, smoking and drinking sherry in a packed crowd without really looking at the paintings at all. This might be all right for a bigger and grander scheme involving the press, but their purpose was a modest one, aiming at efficiency in cost. In this last respect, the number of invitation cards to be sent out presented a problem. If they opted for a mere one hundred, this could often fall short of the mark, inasmuch as a snowball effect could ensue, requiring more hastily printed cards for a rush of new potential purchasers. If they over-ordered, on the other hand, costs could easily deflate their profit. A director of a big art gallery had once told them that the number of invitation cards could reach a thousand. If eighty people came, and twenty bought, this would be considered a good exhibition. But supposing eighty people didn't come?

One day Kay found herself in front of the Basil Street Hotel in Knightsbridge. On entering, she was much impressed by the elegance and fine taste of the appointments. It was one of the old kind, with Edwardian mirrors and genuine antiques lining the corridors – the kind rapidly dying out in the world today, and for that reason all the more treasured. She asked to see the manager, requesting the hire of a room for an exhibition of paintings. He was somewhat nonplussed by such an unusual request; but after further discussion he kindly offered her a small area on the first floor, known as the 'Mezzanine Room'. Here in this modest space began an association of Edward's paintings with the Basil Street Hotel which was to last a quarter of a century, beyond the artist's death.

The 'E.F. Wells Exhibitions' were given in this splendid hotel three or four times a year starting in 1950, each one lasting about two weeks. Only watercolours were shown, though occasionally an oil might be included, standing alone on its easel, in case of chance interest on the part of a viewer. The work was usually confined to one region or locality – with titles such as 'Exhibition of West of England Watercolours', or 'Scenes from Italy', and so on; and Edward and Kay rarely departed from this principle.

Sometimes Edward himself would come, sometimes not. To get a rest in the country, they had recently been staying at Westerham in Kent, where that summer of 1950, incidentally, he bade farewell to his step-son for the last time, who was *en route* for a business assignment in the Caribbean. Edward and Kay, meanwhile, now felt more than ever bound by their mutual tie of risk-taking in the uncertain world of art. They had made their stand and there was no turning back. Their hopes were high; it was exciting for Edward to sit in this Mezzanine Room surrounded by his watercolours beautifully framed and hung. It was less like an exhibition, more like a throne room, the culmination of a dream.

They did not start off with a fanfare; they merely announced the first showing in *The Times* and left it at that. This low-key approach scarcely seemed to pay off at first. Viewers were few and sales slow, despite the modest prices aimed at striking a balance between what people could afford and the fine quality of the watercolours. As the possibility of defeat loomed nearer, they hoped for the miracle of a customer coming in and saying, 'I want to buy the whole of that wall!' But such a miracle never occurred, at least not in the beginning. The best that can be said is that during those first exhibitions in the earlier part of 1950, enough was sold to cover expenses, with a little left over for incidentals.

This did not dampen their enthusiasm, however. The luxury of the Basil Street Hotel alone compensated for their lack of immediate success. They were made to feel like wealthy tycoons instead of modest strugglers in the art world, surrounded as they were by perfect staff. Largely responsible for this was the dedication of the hotel manager, Mr Stephen Korany. Responsive to his guests' needs, considerate and highly efficient, he did everything to make the Wells couple feel as comfortable as possible, and they would remember him with warm appreciation.

As the weeks and months went by, the number of visitors slowly began to increase. Collectors also began to find their way to the 'Mezzanine'. Among keen purchasers were Denys Richardson, a professor connected with the Science Museum, Kensington, who bought some of the Italian paintings dating back to 1900. Other purchasers included Mrs Daphne Thomas (later joined by her husband Richard, of Old Church Street, Kensington); Baron and Baroness de Sterzia (whose friendship with Kay continued after the artist's death); C.S. Bright from Chichester; and Anthony Barbour from Bolesworth Castle, near Chester. Mr Barbour, a lawyer, had a penchant for the half-imperial watercolours, as distinct from the slightly smaller 14 × 10 in. and 7 × 10 in. sizes that predominated in these exhibitions.[3]

As their project gathered momentum, there were times when Edward and Kay felt as much happiness for their buyers as the buyers did themselves. There was the day, for example, when a brigadier-general came in with his wife straight from Buckingham Palace, having just received a decoration from the Queen. 'We must celebrate by treating ourselves to a painting,' they said. They chose a watercolour with a strong hue of pink, unusual for an English landscape. It was the side of a farm building reflecting an evening glow, and it stood out among the other landscape colours on the wall, where green predominated. Edward and Kay were sorry to part with it. But this was eclipsed by the happiness they felt for their discerning purchasers – two contented people on an auspicious occasion taking a painting to what was surely the perfect home for it, somewhere in Hampshire.

Another thrill was the day they received a telegram from a businessman announcing he was coming to the exhibition by aeroplane. He duly arrived and bought a fine drawing called *Early Morning on the Derwent*, painted by Edward in Derbyshire. He imparted good cheer and euphoria to all around him and was immensely delighted with his purchase. Unable to forget the unusual incident, Kay many years later tried to buy it back, as with others. But such attempts usually met with a polite refusal. Such an approach often puts a buyer on his or her guard, reasoning, usually rightly, that the work must have appreciated in value. One notable exception was Edward's *Holne Bridge*, the famous picturesque bridge in Devon. Here the purchaser kindly agreed to sell back the painting only because she was going blind.

On another occasion Lord Stavordale, occupant of Melbury House at Evershot, came in and here too was a delightful encounter. Many years ago Edward had painted a large-size work of Melbury Park, the seat of the Ilchester family. The artist was on familiar ground here. The deer he depicted, grouped and alert, stood on one side of the canvas, close by the famous Melbury trees in all their primeval splendour. In a fit of whimsy rooting back to a seventeenth-century custom, Edward had painted himself in the picture, toiling up the long winding path to Melbury House bearing his easel and paints. He knew that path well. As a child he had often gone to play with the Ilchester children, and later he had been a guest at their house. Kay and Edward now wrote to Lord Stavordale, telling him of the existence of the painting and suggesting its sale. The latter replied that he would like to see it, but that he doubted whether he would want to buy it as there were so many paintings at Melbury House already. When he came and saw it, however, he was enchanted: 'It is beautifully painted. I would like it for my daughter. Will you sell it to me?' The manner of the request, implying that it was the artist who was doing the honour in consenting to part with it, typified the courtesy of this gracious patron. A price was agreed; and the painting duly came into the possession of his (late) daughter, Lady Teresa Agnew, at Melbury House.

Americans were particularly infectious with their enthusiasm. An unforgettable visitor was a young broker from New York. At first glance he was not

Melbury Park, Dorset

the sort of man with whom one would associate a love for English landscape. But after walking around the exhibition room several times, he suddenly sat down and buried his face in his hands, seemingly in emotional distress. Astounded, Edward and Kay asked him what was the matter. 'Please forgive me,' he replied, 'I find this work so expressive of the inexpressible in nature that I am overwhelmed.' Praise indeed, albeit on a rather dramatic note! Without more ado he chose five watercolours of England, landscapes without incident, for his home in New York – each painting, as he put it, to adorn each of the five rooms there. Champagne followed, needless to say; for these purchases approached the miracle they had long been hoping for in terms of a whole wall 'disappearing' in one fell swoop.

Another American, among many, was a tall, elderly, and well-groomed man-about-town, courtly and cosmopolitan in manner. He asked for a 'cool, quiet, clean English watercolour' to take back as a present for his wife. Kay was just about to get out their portfolio to show him some of the more austere paintings when he suddenly caught sight of a small oil panel portraying a nude girl in half-light which they had stood on its easel that very morning. Mysterious, challenging, almost impish, the work was titled simply *Nymph*. He soon forgot all about the 'cool, quiet, clean English watercolour' and left the Mezzanine Room positively delighted, the *Nymph* tucked squarely under his arm. They rejoiced at his happiness; as Edward said wickedly, 'I hope his wife will like it too!' It was one of the few oils they included for viewing in this setting, among the quickest to be sold, and Edward and Kay often pondered on its destiny.

Such dealings did not always go so smoothly. A somewhat intriguing visitor was a beautiful and expensive lady who selected with sure touch two of their very best half-imperial watercolours. But the next day the lady returned with her husband, an elderly man who strode into the room, red-faced, to announce, 'My wife had no business whatever to buy these two expensive watercolours without first consulting me!' And he was about to demand his money back. The Wells couple were nonplussed at being faced with such a situation, one they had not experienced before. They did the right thing, as it turned out, by suggesting a return of the cheque in exchange for the paintings. The man began to melt in front of Edward, then stared at Kay, as his wife suddenly put in with the remark, 'I told you if you could only just meet the artist and his wife, you wouldn't demur!' Reflecting on her comment afterwards, they noted how humbled the man looked in the presence of all three. He deeply apologized for being so unpleasant, and absolutely refused to part with the watercolours.

Another memorable visitor was a certain army major who came in with much aplomb, seeking a present for his fiancée. He was tall, dark, and handsome, a veritable Adonis. He said his fiancée was incredibly beautiful, and that he was indeed fortunate to be her's. 'She has romance on her eyelashes,' he went on, quoting from George Meredith. He chose two fine watercolours, one of them painted at Bradford Peverell in Dorset. On being promised they would receive a cheque in due course, they decided to trust him and allowed him to walk away with the paintings. But no word came. Anxiously, they sent him a polite reminder; and a few days later to their great relief, he returned. Gone was the aplomb, however, as on his first appearance. With a hangdog look, bearing the pictures under his arm, he said his fiancée had broken off the engagement and would they be so kind as to take the watercolours back. Whatever his true motive, they obliged, especially as he looked crestfallen; they often wondered what happened to him and to the siren who had failed him. Edward and Kay were arguably foolish for having trusted him in the first place; but they were gaining experience and learning when it might be expedient to bend the rules and make exceptions. They had recognized his sincerity instinctively. But there was one occasion when a customer got his way even when instincts told otherwise.

This concerned a man who said he was flying over to Switzerland to stay with his mother. He was smallish, dapper, well-dressed and well-spoken, with peculiar eyes, dark and piercing. Kay was alone in the room on this occasion, and felt vaguely uneasy. The exhibition was of Switzerland, and he chose two pleasant scenes – *Lake Geneva* and *Arosa*. He produced his cheque-book, asking Kay as he did so whether she could very kindly give him £20 in change if he made out the cheque with this amount added to the price of the paintings. He said that the banks were not yet open and he was anxious to reach Heathrow airport as quickly as possible to catch his plane. Against her better judgement, Kay complied. The cheque of course turned out to be a bad one. But she only lost the money and happily not the paintings, which had not yet been sent on. Kay felt abashed, nevertheless, at having been so easily duped, and Mr Korany, the hotel manager had to reassure her that she did not need to feel put out as petty criminals like this one were commonplace, especially in places like hotels.

As time went on a huge number of interesting people from all walks of life and nationalities came to the exhibitions, and letters of appreciation came in from purchasers and admirers all over the world. These tributes were manna to Edward and Kay in moments of low morale, whenever the pace of an exhibition was slow. As with all enterprises, there were ups and downs, and in this respect, perhaps it is fitting to end with an 'up'. Such moments approached the miracle they had been hoping for and which had eluded them for a long time. One opening day a Mr T.E. Johnson came in and bought six watercolours all at once. It was such a splendid and unexpected surprise for the first day of an exhibition – approaching the miracle that had eluded them for some time – that they inordinately celebrated with champagne.

Edward, now in his seventy-sixth year, was beginning to feel tired; but even at this late stage he could wrestle with a portrait patiently and bring it to perfection despite the sitter being fidgety and difficult. Such a man was Sir William Gavin of Upper Belgrave Street. Extremely busy, unable to relax, Sir William was candid enought to admit his own shortcoming:

> I always meant to pay you [the full agreed amount] if the portrait turned out well, so here is the [further sum] I owe you. Thank you so much for all your courtesy and trouble on an unsatisfactory patient!
>
> All good wishes,
> Yours sincerely,
> William Gavin[4]

This was Edward's last portrait (completed, incidentally, at about the same time as King George VI opened the Festival of Britain in May 1951), yet he still looked forward to those days when he could attend the exhibitions periodically given at the Basil Street Hotel. Brisk or slow as they may be, he found them intriguing. Each visit was different, one never knew who was coming or what was to be the destiny of any of his watercolours. Increasingly, however, he felt constrained to stay at home in their flat in Cadogan Place. He would forage among his collection of books, pore over crosswords in *The Times* or the *Daily Telegraph*, listen to concerts on the wireless. He liked Kay to be near him, sketch-book always at hand, literally in his pocket, so as to touch off a drawing of her, or of any passing theme which interested him.

By August 1952 they had moved to 39 Sloane Gardens, following the expiration of their lease. 'This is where we came in, Kay,' Edward had said, recalling 39 Parkhill Road, the place where his second life had really begun. Perhaps he sensed that this address would be his last. Only a short while later, he drew an outline of Kay, bringing the sketch to life with special dedication – the last effort he ever made. It was the end of a long story. And through all the peaks and setbacks, happiness and personal tragedies, the hints of fame, deprivations of war, health and illnesses, through all the chapters of his crowded years and the reigns of six monarchs from Victoria to Elizabeth II, Edward had made his story rich and varied. Despite faults here and there, he had led a fulfilled, unselfish life, never complaining when things went wrong – whenever the art world was dead or disappointing, or in moments of personal adversity. Sustaining him in this was his wife's tireless devotion to his cause. And Edward appreciated her support. He always needed personal company, and could never live on his own, at least not for long.

It was a beautiful day that morning of 19 August, with blue sky and sunshine everywhere. Edward had dressed early on this occasion, earlier in fact than Kay, normally the first to rise, who was feeling unwell. After breakfast he sat by her side, quiet and withdrawn, seeming far away, almost transparent. An important letter had to be sent; and as it was such a fine day and the pillar-box was nearby, she asked him if he would post it. He looked well enough, as if he might enjoy the outing, even though the doctors had already warned him never to go out unattended. As he left their bedroom he said softly, 'I won't be long.' These were his last words. Untypically, he left off his pocket-watch on the way out.

The minutes went by, and then more minutes. They seemed to get louder in the gathering silence, emphasizing the ticking of the watch. Another fifteen minutes and Kay became alarmed. Throwing on her outdoor clothes, she anxiously walked toward Sloane Square to meet him. But there was no sign of him as people went about their usual business. Now desperate, she approached a policeman. On being informed that her husband, elderly and delicate, had gone out half an hour before and had not returned, he went to a police-box; and then they took Kay to St George's Hospital. The ambulance men reported that Edward had collapsed near Sloane Square Underground station. Attempts to revive him in the ambulance had been futile. Kay, on being given a sedative in the hospital, could just recognise their family doctor, Montague-Smith, standing over her and pronouncing that Edward was dead.

She had him taken to Dorset and saw him laid near his father in the grounds of the little church of St Osmond's in Evershot – the place where he had been nurtured. Close by, just visible, was the roof-top of his happy childhood home.

Centuries ago someone said of Calderón, the great Spanish dramatist and poet, that 'he died like a swan, singing'. Edward, too, in a different way, at a different time, had joined his company.

CHAPTER NINE

POSTSCRIPT IN WESSEX AND WESTPHALIA

Two people were primarily responsible for reviving public interest in Edward's work after his death: the artist's widow, Kay herself, and Edward's principal collector, Peter Scheiwe. This part deals with the former, with particular reference to the 1950s and 1960s.

After a comforting visit to her son in Mexico, Kay returned to England in 1953 and rented the wing of a manor house near Dorchester. Far from succumbing to a life of seclusion, she decided at this point to continue promoting her husband's work. Accordingly, with little help from anyone, she arranged a series of exhibitions of his watercolours dealing mainly with West Country subjects which she presented in towns in that area. With portfolios of his paintings under her arm and the frames in bundles, Kay determinedly visited a number of such towns from 1954 to the early 1960s, giving one-man exhibitions of his work usually lasting a fortnight. These included shows at Dorchester (which she visited several times, giving the exhibition at Judge Jeffrey's lodgings), Bridport (at the Museum and Art Gallery), Taunton (at the Castle Hotel), Exeter (at the Rougemont Hotel), Yeovil (at the Three Choughs), Salisbury (at the White Hart), Winchester (at the Royal Hotel), Bournemouth (at the Royal Bath Hotel), and Bath (in the Pump Room), in more or less this order. It was a burdensome task, but the effort was worth while. A great many works were presented at these exhibitions, including the following: *A Winter's Aftermath* (where a bent old man stands by some haystacks on his farmstead, as if poised between the long haul of winter and the first buds of spring), *Storm over Hardy Country*, *Lulworth Heath*, *Elms in Mist* (shown many years before at the Royal Institute of Painters in Water Colours), *Cows in Meadow* (done at Bradford Peverell and shown many years before at the Royal Institute of Oil Painters), *Reflections*, *Hampshire*, and scenes of Dartmoor and the Cornish coast. Almost without exception, there was a marked enthusiasm as well as a good press – very different from some of her previous attempts with her husband in earlier wartime years. Apart from her own efforts, this enthusiasm was doubtless due to the residue of local interest among patrons and acquaintances in the west of England who personally remembered the name of Edward Francis Wells. The frequent and cordial receptions which Kay received, moreover, served to ease her own transition from a state of obvious grief to one of purposeful activity in a real world. So much so, that in time she was able to organize 'E.F. Wells Exhibitions' in other parts of the country, including London.

A minute sample list of purchasers at these exhibitions would include: Charles Wallis of Gillingham; Harold Carter of Warminster, who bought *Winter's Aftermath* at a Salisbury exhibition; Lois Munro of Brunswick Square, London, who bought *Ruins of Bindon Abbey, Wool*; and Gertrude McHardy, who bought *The River Frome.*[1] Some would select paintings sent on approval from London, such as Margaret Wray of Taunton, who kept some Cornish scenes with a green and turquoise sea under a threatening sky; while Gerald and Hanna de Boynville of Walkern Hall, Hertfordshire, bought the superb *River Dart* independently of the exhibitions.

Reviews seemed to reflect the enthusiasm of buyers. One example was the following press notice in the *Western Gazette* of an exhibition given in Dorchester in November 1954, which is typical of many. It was written by Val Orrin, who discerned the poetic nuances underlying Edward's work:

> The first exhibition of paintings by Edward Francis Wells to be held in the West Country for 20 years is an event of considerable interest and importance to all those with pretensions to the knowledge of art. Wells, who died two years ago at the age of 76, was one of the finest watercolour artists the West has ever produced, and it was on the hills and dales and on the windswept heaths and mellow lanes of the western counties that his finest work was done. . . . As a youth he wandered through the villages of Dorset, Somerset and Devon, painting almost with feverish haste all the strange compositions of nature that stimulated his poetic soul. The mist-shrouded downs, the moors with their host of half-seen, sombre colours are some of the finest of all English watercolours. But it is only now since his death that his full stature has been recognized, though during his lifetime his works were exhibited at several leading galleries – the Royal Academy, the Hibernian Gallery, and Bradford Municipal Art Gallery, among others. Now his paintings are increasingly sought after by discerning collectors. The exhibition in Dorchester . . . has been specially collected by his second wife Katharine, whom Wells married in 1935. The collection she has gathered is small, but representative. There are studies from his youth, from the experimental period of his middle years, and examples of his full towering maturity with such works as *Elms in Mist* and *Purbeck*. Both these works expound the greatest technical skill in draughtsmanship, but it is the pathos of the desolate scene that appeals. The colour has to be sought for, and the entire composition is simple in the extreme. There are in these two paintings all the lonely majesty of the winter season. Not that Wells's works

are sombre, for in many sketches he has captured the transparent delicacy of spring and the full richness of high summer. But it is when the autumn winds take the first leaves from the trees, and a mellow nostalgia comes slowly over the earth towards the long, sad English winter that Wells comes into his own world. With passionate simplicity he loved landscape – landscape without incident, for often in his work nothing detracts from the full visual panorama.

It is, perhaps, a pity that there are not any of his magnificent portraits on view, for during his lifetime he painted many great families, and today there are few manors in the West that do not boast of at least one Wells in their gallery . . . The West Country can be proud to have been the stimulating influence in the art of this great traditionalist.'[2]

The same sentiment is expressed in a similar review of an exhibition given at Yeovil in 1957, which also appeared in the *Western Gazette*:

The countryside always possesses a certain quality of beauty, whatever the season, sometimes still and at others wild. Wells, a master of colour technique (although sparing in his use of colour) and the effects of nature, could capture the feeling of these changes with his quick unfaltering brush. At times he uses bold imaginative strokes, giving a sense of urgency and power, and then he shows a sensitivity which marks him as a great artist and his work a poem in colour. In this exhibition the viewer is taken through the changes of the day from *Early Morning on the Hillside*, where the mists are being dispelled by the first rays of the sun on a hill at Evershot through *Midsummer on the Downs*, in which the artist has captured the feeling of the simmering afternoon heat, to a remarkable evening scene of *Melbury Park and Melbury House*. In this particular piece is shown his amazing sense of perspective in a picture which seems to radiate life and warmth. But not only the changes of the day captivated his imagination; the seasons, too, were ever ready material for the brush which scarcely left his hand.

Perhaps the most magnificent piece in this exhibition is a picture of *The River Dart in Spate*. Here one can see vividly the urgency of the sparkling foaming waters hurrying through the leafy trees in a race to be first to the sea. *Edge of the Moor* depicts the bleakness of nature when the high winds arrive, and in *Storm over Hardy Country* Wells, with a velvety touch, brings out all the terrifying grandeur of the evening storm as it looms over the hills.

This is an exhibition which should not be missed by art lovers. Mrs Wells attributes much of her late husband's success to the fact that he would never let himself be satisfied with his work, but perhaps it was also due to the fact he had the wisdom to realize that one cannot improve on nature.

A.C.B.[3]

The second person largely responsible for fostering interest in Edward's work, Mr Peter Scheiwe, hails from Münster, Westphalia, in West Germany. This important city harbours the huge timber works of Ostermann and Scheiwe, of which Peter is owner and chief director. Dedicated to reconstruction from the ruins of 1945, this region from the Rhine to the Ruhr shared in the *Wirtschaftswunder*, or 'economic miracle', of German recovery. During this time Peter was searching wider horizons of cultural interest, and a chance visit to a London exhibition of Edward Wells's pictures helped him realize this goal.

Kay herself was promoting this exhibition. After her rewarding experience in the counties, she moved to London, specifically to Knightsbridge, where she had spent the last years with her husband. Thus it was the Basil Street Hotel which she visited once more. The exhibitions she gave there, albeit with the absence of the artist, were frequented by a growing clientele, among whom the foremost collector became Peter Scheiwe himself.

On an ordinary day in 1964 this unassuming Westphalian came casually in. He was alone in the gallery – the same Mezzanine Room as in previous years – and walked silently around, examining everything. It was an exhibition of drawings done in Italy at the turn of the century; and the first E.F. Wells work he ever acquired was *The Cypress Walk to the Villa d'Este*, a delightful sepia drawing. This was the beginning of a long and continuing association with the artist's work. The only son of a distinguished family of industrialists, Peter had developed at an early age a deep appreciation for the arts. He took to Edward's work in a big way and now has a substantial collection of his paintings at his homes in Westphalia and Switzerland. While knowledgeable, his tastes are simple. Yet on looking at a painting, he sees at once the extent of an artist's inspiration and the trend of his direction. His one regret is that he never had an opportunity to meet Edward in person. And to the extent that he is never swayed by dictatorial taste or packaged commercialism in art, he and Edward would have shared a common bond.

Among the considerable number of Wells canvasses which Peter Scheiwe has purchased, only a few can be mentioned: *Interior at Evershot, Return to the Cottage, Madame Bravet, Iris and Wistaria, Mimosa, Bathers on the Norfolk Broads, Portrait of the Artist's Father, The Sapphic Ode, Repose, Flowers on the Piano, Children Under a Japanese Umbrella* (Judith and Sylvia), and *Self-Portrait of the Artist*. A recent purchase is *The Path to the Winnatts*, a beauty spot near Castleton in Derbyshire. While hard put to part with them, Kay saw in this growing private collection an ideal chance for their security. Here was a man who loved the work, and who would look after it and do his best to promote it. Its ultimate well-being remained the prime concern of both.

So many E.F. Wells canvasses now hang in the Scheiwe homes, from oils to bright watercolours, their supple texture blending perfectly with the furniture and interior design, that few would deny the transition has been a great success. Edward himself would have found it a decided blessing – his own 'children', as it were, in good safe hands.

Not far from this cosmopolitan city of Münster, moreover, Peter Scheiwe and his friends organized a successful public exhibition of E.F. Wells paintings in 1989. In this age of the European Community, with its economic and cultural links, when cities from Münster to Manchester are 'twinned' with another to mark a special civic relationship, it is a fitting distinction that Edward's work was singled out to further this bond. It also reflects the discerning insight of the sponsor. For the visual arts, especially in their panoramic context, play a unique role in bringing national heritages together.

CHAPTER TEN

APPRAISAL

What are the merits of Edward as an artist, and what are his drawbacks? These are difficult questions to answer, since both critics and artists see things in different lights. A starting-point is to say that Edward Francis Wells has been neglected far too long. But this to some extent was his own fault. There was something very modest and unassuming about the man. So much so, that while caring inwardly that the world may one day recognize his talent and proclaim his art, he appeared not to care enough openly to try and achieve these ends.

One example of his detachment was his devotion to the countryside. At Evershot he had developed an innate perceptiveness for nature. Essentially a rural man, like the young Shakespeare, perhaps, whose quotations he always carried in his pocket, he loved nature in its mutability and calm. His landscapes have a silent strength, his images a ring of joy, which nature itself often divulges. He knew, after all, what he was about. He hadn't studied Titian or Turner for nothing.

Yet despite his diligent pursuit of the Old Masters, there was something that put Edward in a class by himself. He was forthright in his execution, with bold brushwork pleasing to the eye, and it is out of such boldness that harmony is made; but something else lurks here that makes his achievement so outstanding. With watercolours, for example, as mentioned earlier, he knew exactly the right moment to strike the moistened paper with his brush, so that his colours have a fluid softness about them which his measured skill has wrought. This 'soft-like' quality has a breath of life to it, achieving the effect of what Matthew Arnold described as 'sweetness and light', something you find in music also. Edward always sought that mystical meeting-point between shape and sound, conceding music to be the highest form of art. Thus his watercolours have a poignancy all their own. From Dorset to Derbyshire, from the Pyrenees to Switzerland they cover a wide range – the products of a sensitive imagination; they have an open-air immediacy, and suggest perfect identity with nature. Indeed, one might detect the influence of Francis Thompson and his 'filigree petal' theme.

He knew, then, how to lend colour to a landscape and thus give it a permanent poetic life in a way a poet does with word or sound. Yet the very simplicity of his designs masks a deeper complexity in a conceptual sense, which is often the essence of great art. His deep communion with nature was not just decorative or repetitious. He took it so much to heart that once his watercolours had been, as it were, inducted with the breath of life, they continued to live. Edward's scenes, moreover, are like microcosms, implying something larger, permitting the viewer to stretch the canvas with his own imagination. The jewels of his Italian sketches suffice as good examples. They seem part of a larger tracery of mythology and history which one never tires of looking at. There is a touch of Tiepolo in them. They are lyrical and pastoral – fluid yet restful at the same time. With his works in general you can feel the suggestion of movement (as with his approaching windstorms), leading to that supreme moment of 'libation to the gods' which his art suggests, though sometimes after a hard struggle. Obversely, there is often a hinted aftermath, or stilled after-effect, as with a hawthorn tree bent by the wind – a breaking away from that supreme moment of 'libation'. The Greeks had this gift. But in the process Edward knew that the facets of nature can play strange tricks, knew the harsh reality that lurks behind. Thus with his larger works, perhaps, there is a starker chiaroscuro – more light and darkness, point and counterpoint, even as the crudeness of life, the cruelty, is ignored. For it is the positive aspect of nature he chose to preserve. He aimed at 'pristine' truth, not 'ugly' or 'distorted' truth; and in his attempt to preserve realism on whatever scale, he wished his works to be a feast for the eye, an expression of soul. For Edward, there could be no evil here; and this applied to humankind as well.

With his portraiture however, as distinct from his watercolours or land-scapes in oil, there was a limitation in that the sometimes stiff postures were necessarily at the dictate of his patrons. Even so, the same 'soft-like' quality prevails. And with many of his greater, more personal works in oil – the studies of his two wives for example (*The Sapphic Ode* and *Portrait of Kay*) – there is a compelling nuance in the expressions, an aura imparted to the whole, that makes them singularly arresting. The flesh tones are lifelike and the pose is in perfect harmony with the design. Here he displays his mastery ·of technique superlatively. This mastery thrived when he painted portraits entirely for personal ends. Then he was aroused and inspired.

It is only a pity that Edward did not try to project his work more widely to the outside world. For, despite the popularity of Cubism, Surrealism, and other experiments of those decades, there is no reason why the world could not have picked up at least part of his message. Yet in a way his very detachment was what his art was all about, with perhaps a touch of stubbornness, or indifference, where public relations were concerned. And not without a plausible reason. In the changing world of the twentieth century, which he fully understood, Edward stuck to his own terms, reflecting nature and humanity as he saw them. These for him were changeless standards, part of the unchanging verities. He could brook no compromise with what he regarded as mediocrity. Nor would he stray outside his compass. Innocence, wildness, sadness, joy, rebirth, remembrance constituted his creed, at least where landscape painting was concerned, and some of these qualities appear in his portraits as well.

The quality of innocence, for example, is nowhere better expressed than in his portraits of children. 'They sweeten labour,' as one philosopher noted. Edward was a past master at capturing that look of fleeting innocence in children's faces – difficult because it is so fleeting. One recalls an oil study of his daughter Judith in a drifting white dress, whose look seems to be asking why she has been deposited on this earth. Another is of Vivien – an infant just awakened, with sleep still encasing her, the head with dewy eyes set amid the delicate tracery of her pillow and bib. The result, *A Baby Awakened*, is an oil study of exquisite translucence. As his sitters get older, Edward still tried to preserve something of that pristine innocence which every parent likes to see in his or her offspring. There is the charming oil mentioned in a previous context, entitled *The Young Ballerina*, of Marlys, aged about nine, with her white frou-frou ballet dress ringed with thistle-down skirt, and white satin slippers ready to dance before the eye. Indeed, a copy of this is believed to have been made for an admirer. Altogether Edward painted about forty children in his working life. His own son Bill, Lady Forbes's son, Lady Boyne's son, Lady Romayne Cecil, Mary Rose Pellew – these were just some of the subjects.

Edward was circumscribed, as has been said, by the limits of his profession. A patron who commissions a portrait wants a likeness of the sitter, not just an impression conveyed by the artist. His portraits, therefore, are first a likeness, with the desired posture often a difficult matter to negotiate, and only then could he concentrate on anything further. In short, an aura conveyed by an expression had to be secondary. With this limitation, Edward preferred young people as sitters. Unlike adults, they did not fuss about untidy hair or clothes, were often less self-conscious, and showed interest in the artist's brushes and palette. Their mouths furthermore were fairly easy features for him to portray, being more relaxed than the stiffness of a maturer face. With an adult portrait, by contrast, the mouth for Edward became the most difficult feature of all, in which the slightest movement by the sitter or the slightest touch on the part of the artist could alter the whole expression. Indeed, this feature could be a pointer to the whole character of a subject. Hands for Edward were also difficult. The intricacy of the palm, with its mounts and revealing lines of shadow, was a more complex task for him to draw than the eyes, which, unlike some other artists, he found he could portray with relative ease, even more so with children.

While both sexes featured fairly evenly among Edward's professional commissions, in his opinion men made the worst sitters. And elderly men at

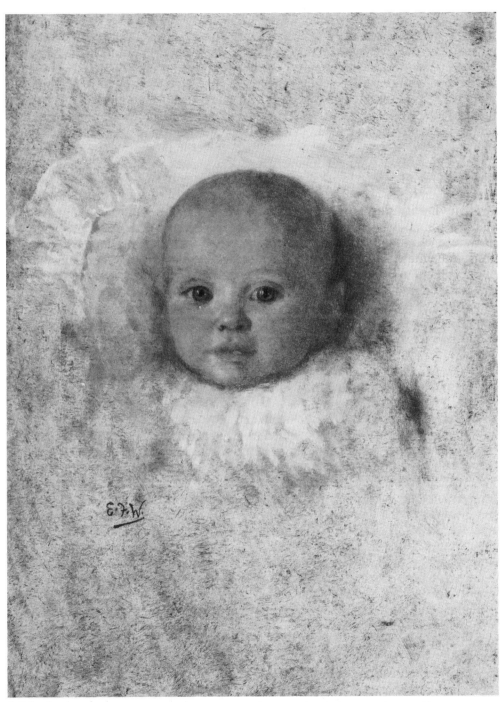

A Baby Awakened

that. They would often fuss about their hair or necktie, would demand which profile was better, or ask, 'Should it be full face?' Yet despite his sometimes critical approach to sitters, Edward was a charitable man and his comments should be taken in their context. For, as we have seen, he underwent a lot of frustration in his professional life.

In other ways too he had to accommodate himself to the whims and fancies of his hosts. ('Don't forget rod and racket,' as one kind host enjoined). Partaking in the lavish house parties frequently given by county families, however, was often a burden to Edward, who, while at least liking tennis, was somewhat withdrawn. He also tended to shun the company of colleagues, so that his friends were few, though close. In a word, he was neither social-minded nor gregarious, but reserved. In later years, however, Edward regretted his isolation from the mainstream of the art world, self-imposed as it was, which cost him dear in terms of advancing his cause. He could easily have tried for RA status, for example, but by then it was too late. Politics of this sort was not his forte.

Edward had other shortcomings which are worth examining here, if only because understanding Edward the man helps one to understand his art. He lacked astuteness in money matters, for example. Though not rare among artists, this had some bearing on his professional life. True, he had a trust fund to protect him, but though he understood the importance of smaller pennies, he wasn't very wise with the larger pounds. He could calmly live on capital and sell good property imprudently, thus depriving himself of future revenue. The result was more dependence on professional work to pay his way, some of which he disliked for the reasons given above. On other occasions, perhaps because of deeper money worries, he could be unnecessarily finicky. He is known to have engaged in lengthy correspondence with a furniture remover for allegedly having gone over his estimate (can we blame Edward here?), while he once rebuked a workman for having a cigarette in his mouth when present in his drawing-room. But such rebukes were rare.

In a sense he was a contradictory character. But the contradictions were more apparent than real. He was formal and reserved, for example, letting others do the talking, which suggested, if not a lack of interest, then a cold detachment; and he could be almost caustic when he did admonish someone, which suggested he was stiff and unapproachable. All these 'suggestions' were deceptive. The real Edward, distinct from the apparent Edward, was rather the opposite. He was very communicative once you got to know him, and very knowledgeable without being condescending. He may have been a stickler for good manners but was warm and intimate to those whom he considered sincere. Indeed, he would gladly teach others what he could if they really wanted to learn. His assumed unapproachability was in fact a sort of mask – partly the product of his staid upbringing, but chiefly a defence by which he isolated himself from superficialities. We have already seen him ill at ease with purely social life. Trivia indeed bored him. But once the mask was penetrated he was outspokenly human – guffawing at others' jokes as well as his own and readily warming up to conversationalists.

A generous quality was his willingness to be self-critical, even to laugh at himself. Few have this modesty. Once, when it was suggested that a book be written about him, and someone asked whether anyone would read it, Edward retorted with a roar of laughter, 'Quite so! Who's going to read it!'

He certainly hid his talents under a bushel, but in other respects he was fun-loving and witty, at least with his intimates. Though he may have been ascetic in moments of despair, as a husband he was indulgent and indulging, giving the best of himself to both his wives. He also had immense spiritual reserves. Disliking mediocrity and humbug, he never complained when things went wrong, judging others magnanimously and giving them the benefit of the doubt.

Margaret Sinclair, author of a book on Charles Williams and editor of an Anglican magazine, whom Edward painted, had this to say about him: 'He is a peacemaker, courteous, with perfect manners, but not at the expense of fidelity or principle. As to the deftness with which he uses his hands, they are immensely sensitive, gentle but firm. He is a thoughtful man, content in later life to sit for long among his favourite books – one guesses he is deeply spiritual.'[1] Such comments foreshadowed the many condolences to follow at his death when letters poured in from every quarter. Families from the Exmouths to the Exeters, indeed from all walks of life, remembered him.

Today many of his pictures hang in unexpected places, or lie stored in secret vaults. Their multifariousness testifies to his versatility in both medium and genre, but their one common factor is true-tone imagery. Indeed, the further time moves on, the more 'classic' and 'realist' his work becomes. Essentially a product of pre-1914 England, Edward fought a losing battle for a style that did not change markedly enough for it to keep abreast of the shifting values of our time. In short, his style went out of date too fast. But what a style it was! When all is said and done, what works by other artists of the early twentieth century have the delicacy of his sepia drawings, his pen-and-ink sketches of Italy, his cycle of Italian watercolours, his French Basque scenes or those of Switzerland, his flower pieces, his early pastel portraits (Edward was at home in almost any medium), his watercolours of the English landscape, to say nothing of his magnificent works in oil? Here, perhaps, in his Italian and English watercolours, we see Edward at his best. And the same would apply on a grander scale among the oils to *Milking Time* and *Wareham Heath*, to *The Shower of Gold* or *Repose*.

What, then, can we say of all his portraits? If comparisons must be made, his landscapes outshine, perhaps, the general level of his portraits, but with this proviso: that a few of his very best portraits outshine anything else he did. One has only to recall that of *Toshio Urabe*, or that of *Doris Bowyer*, or his *Kay as a Dancer* to get an idea of his astonishing mastery of style when truly inspired. The secret of this inspiration stems from his study of others, chiefly the Old Masters, of nature and of true-tone imagery (with much hard work in the process). And the end-product was essentially his own. If critics see the influence of Titian or Thomas Lawrence or Robert Wilson in his work, so be it, but none would be able to identify any point at which Edward lifted another's technique and made it his own. Influence is not the same as plagiarism. The latter, of course, can reach all levels of artist, even if mainly practised by the mediocre. Edward, of course, was not mediocre, neither did he plagiarize (unless it be from nature itself). His inspiration and perceptions were positive and personal. Each of his works is *sui generis*, revealing a pattern, a keenly-felt vision all its own, a world within a world, yet fusing with it; a product of the imagination.

It is sometimes said of Edward that if he had widened his scope from merely drawing the attention of the public to what he had already done 'inside' his world to including more touches of the real world outside – changing after the 1920s so rapidly that it bore little resemblance to what had gone before – he could have become a truly popular artist. Perhaps there is a germ of truth in this. One is mindful of Turner with his iron ships and steam trains. Aware of this criticism, Edward preferred to regard it as applying to his own chosen limits, rather than to his own limitations. One feels he could so easily have portrayed humanity in all its suffering, for example (which is what Europe largely went through from 1914 to the 1940s) – the horrors in the trenches, beggars in the streets during the Depression, the Blitz on London, soldiers and their girlfriends huddled in shelters, with heaps of ruin around them. All this, however, was simply not his choice. His work was limited by its subject matter, not by want of inspiration. Choice is the artist's privilege, he would have argued. Why should he stray outside a given range? Refusing to adapt his technique to the technology of a changing world, he purposely confined himself to the poetic realism of the subjects he preferred, like a taskmaster concentrating on a discipline. Bach, it will be noted, did the same in regard to his own pure brand of absolute music (in between his bouts of organ-testing), and was already looked upon as rather baroque and outmoded in his own day. Yet do we downgrade his work because, unlike Handel, he ignored the lure of popular appeal?

In shunning the avant-garde Edward never affected to be priggish. He only condemned those whom he considered charlatans, of whatever school they belonged to. Moreover, within the limits he had set himself he was less restricted than he appeared to be. As a matter of record he did include considerable touches of the 'real' world about him – from workmen (as in his *Tithe Barn, Cerne Abbas*), farmers, roving labourers, bathers and skaters to the buzz bomb of the Second World War. As one commentator put it long ago: 'Wells usually grips Nature completely and has no hesitancy in showing his grasp of her essentials and her passing mood. *Tea in the Hayfield* [and others] are all good, but are not so much pure Nature as he is wont to treat – they all suggest immediate connection with humanity, and perhaps for that reason

Tithe Barn, Cerne Abbas

will be more appreciated by the general public.'[2] Edward could also suggest narrative on his canvas. As he would have argued, though, it is not necessarily the function of the artist to record only what people want. He hated the dictation of norms and the fickleness of fashion. 'An artist', he once said, 'should first know how to draw; then, guided by his own instincts, should be as free as the wind.' In his view what might be called 'the concrete realism of nature', set apart from any age or any critic, had as much claim to artistic representation as any other style, and gave his work a sense of detachment from the world of human change.

Ironically, it is not so much the changing world as the world before it changed so dramatically in 1914 that arouses interest today. The spate of books and films on the subject testifies to this. His work, for instance, of the 1930s, may not be the current coin of dealers (unless perhaps it be a French or Spanish work), but as every dealer knows, the climate of the market swiftly changes. Edward's judgement about the artist's independence from the dictates of fashion might eventually come full circle in his favour, for his own inner world, along with its reverence for the Old Master tradition, archaic as it may have seemed in the 1930s, may well become aesthetically permissible during the 1990s, by reflecting an earlier age than the immediate past.

Favouring Edward's cause, it is plausible to argue that realism is already coming back into fashion. One has only to look at America for example, where painters like William Bailey and a host of others are forging new paths on realism's behalf. Nature, highways, conurbations, or just stations, airports, apartments, pretty girls dressing or undressed – each and every one of these facets of the artist's vision has validity, without abstractions or distortions. To each his own, Edward would have argued, provided there is sincerity of purpose.

Regardless of how high posterity will rank him, to make it clear that Edward ranks high by any standards has been a purpose of this book. Despising crass commercialism and mass-produced judgements, and in refusing to join any articulate group, he remained a loner. His very apartness made him singular. Self contained without being self-effacing, humble but without sacrificing his principles, Edward, in clinging to his dreams – more tangibly in clinging to the great 'Venetian secret' passed down to him and which he worked on to improve – expressed his awe both of nature and of the flesh and soul of life.

It is a reverence which he shared with the poets and musicians he admired. It is in their company where his gods are found, from their world that he drew. The buds of spring, the summer heat, the swirling leaves of autumn, melancholy winter – the capricious moods of all the seasons, whether storm or breeze or mist, and along with them the toiling shapes of humankind – already possessing his imagination many years ago in Dorset, and which (who knows?) were perhaps first aroused in India, are transmuted in his work into a harmonic scale of soft and brilliant colours. His colours dance with delight. Nature has been wedded to the history of a time. Innocence, wildness, sadness, joy, rebirth, remembrance – such themes recur in all his work. But perhaps the greatest quality he has given us is remembrance.

APPENDIX I

THE 'VENETIAN SECRET' AND 'TRUE-TONE PAINTING'

Howley Wells's theory of luminosity and scale of illumination for adjusting colours to the vertical plane

In referring to sunlight Howley Wells wrote:

'There is the same fixed relation of illumination between the highest white illuminated cloud near the sun when reflected down to earth and 'white in sunlight' on earth, as there is between 'white in sunlight' on earth and 'white' placed at right angles to sunlight. On a grey day there is this same fixed relation between 'white in the sky' represented by the nearest approach to white in its colour and the 'horizontal' representing white in the fullest light. There is the same fixed relation existing between the canvas in full light and the canvas at right angles to full light, viz., a vertical canvas [as in a studio]. This fixed relation of illumination is applicable to all lightings and is represented *by the power of the instrument with the long tube inserted*. . . . Nature's colours are of uneven illumination according to their power of absorbing a scattering light. If all colours were of equal illuminating power to white under the same lighting, it would suffice to raise the illumination of the canvas placed at right angles to full light, up to the fullest light of day, keeping the above relations between earth and sky; but as dark and light colours vary very considerably in illumination power under the same lighting, such a method exaggerates the difference existing in nature between the illuminations of the light and darker colours, making all colours more or less darker compared with white than they should be, and exaggerates the light colours at the expense of the darker ones.'[1]

To set a scale for illumination in colour, Howley Wells applied Abney's table of luminosities, with his instrument graded in power according to his own grouping of the colours into such powers.[2]

Having decided which luminosity of colour and corresponding instrument power an object should be matched to, the artist was given guidelines which Howley Wells spelt out next in his documents. For earth colours on a grey day, for example, he advised that the canvas should be placed vertically, at right angles to full light, and then raised by the instrument according to the required lighting necessary to match the colours, and that all earth colours could thus be matched in their true scale of illumination. In all of this Howley Wells's grouping of the colours into powers could more or less be adhered to. He next gave guidelines to cover sky on a grey day, studio and interior effects, sunlight out of doors, and so on, with the instrument's long or short tube being variously indicated, along with positions for the canvas, whether vertical, horizontal, or tilted. In other respects, the instrument could trace the difference in illumination between the vertical canvas at right angles to sunlight and the vertical canvas in shade when measuring the power of out-of-door sunlight over the effects of a grey day. Similar guidelines followed for studio lighting – 'The full power of white is represented by the long tube on the canvas at right angles to the full light on it, or in the position equal to the difference of lighting on the canvas' – and also for various sky colours, sunsets, and interior effects of all kinds. He then pointed out that colours should be painted under powers below the full lighting of white (according to the luminosity table given in note 2), and that the same power required to match respective colours in light applied also to their respective shadow colours.[3]

Relying heavily on Abney, he dealt with the 'drawing together' of the luminosity between white and black as light is raised on them to the point of extinction, at which point black becomes white. In quoting Abney, 'the same luminosity of white light is necessary to extinguish the same luminosity of all colours almost; and the extinction of every colour is effected by white light, which is seventy-five times brighter than the colour', Howley Wells additionally had in mind the application of his power scale to denote the raising of light on a colour brought into focus by his instrument at full tube. This referred especially to the transfer of the common or true colour on the vertical to canvas, when full light meant one 'power', half-light a half 'power', and so on. A method of adjusting all colours as seen under different angles of lighting to this vertical plane was then given for studio lighting, and then for lighting on a grey day.[4] In the latter case he gave the example where the outdoor vertical was a power above studio vertical, and so the canvas needed to be tipped to below the vertical by one power in order to get the corresponding studio lighting on it. Black in light was double-reflected or matched in full light on this lowered lighting. There were now two powers between black and white to be adjusted as regards the intermediate colours. Eosin dye, being half way, was matched in full light on the vertical canvas. Other colours were matched accordingly between white and black extremes on each side of the half-way colour.

Howley Wells's guidelines for adjusting colours to the vertical plane for studio lighting

'Divide black to white on the vertical into gradations by squares of grey tones each lighter in tone than the last, by a full instrument power. It will be proved that the 6 gradations so made extinguish the colour of black. Do the same with chrome yellow, orange, Eosin dye, emerald green, brown paper, vermillion, cobalt, blue-green, and ultramarine blue. Place them all side by side with the lowest hues of each colour on the bottom row, and it will be seen how their colours are extinguished as they all draw together towards white. We have practically divided by 75 times the brightness of the colours required to extinguish their colour into 6 gradations of light by the instrument. We have now a chess-board arrangement giving practically the tone which every conceivable hue of colour can be matched to as regards tone somewhere on this chess-board.

Now re-arrange this chess-board of colour hues, placing the original colours which started from the vertical against the black & white tones of grey, which, according to Abney, represent their respective luminosity in black and white tone. Scale their gradations of colour already made back & fore towards black & white, and we have a re-arranged chess-board of colours, all truly represented in their black & white tones.

According to Abney, black is 0 and white 100 in luminosity. And therefore every division of the 6 grades between black & white is about $16\frac{1}{2}$. White is 100, chrome yellow 77, orange 63, Eosin dye 45, brown paper 25, emerald green 23, vermillion, blue-green & cobalt 15, ultramarine blue 4.

Place each representative colour in its proper position to the grey tones between black & white in luminosity as given below . . . and grade the tone, backwards & forwards towards black & white as explained above (white at left, black on the vertical at right): white is 100, chrome yellow 84, orange 68, Eosin dye 50 (= black in sunlight on vertical), brown paper & emerald green 33 (= black in light on vertical, grey day, outdoor work), vermillion, blue green & cobalt 16 (= black in light on vertical, studio), ultramarine blue & black 0. The powers of raising for each of the six luminosities (beginning with white, left to right) are 6, 5, 4, 3, 2, & 1 respectively. Six luminosities are given, but probably 3 are quite enough for all practical purposes in transferring from the vertical to canvas.

Every colour & shade of colour is matched in full light & then brought to its common or true colour by being turned to the vertical or the equivalent lighting to the vertical. It is then transferred to canvas according to the position on the matching chess-board hues that it falls under, by swinging the palette between full light & the vertical accordingly. A pointer attached to palette shows the necessary swing of the palette.

Black & ultramarine blue are matched in full light. White in vertical light & the colours between [are matched] according to their luminosity or position on the colour board.'

c. February 1908

Howley Wells's guidelines for preserving the brilliance of original colours when depicted in a lower key after the hue is taken out

'Place the chess-board of colour tints in *full* light of the day wherever a hue in nature matches a tone of the chess-board in illumination that will show the power necessary to bring down the hue of nature on the canvas. The difference between white in *full* light & white on the vertical gives the full power between white & black on the chess board, viz., between the two extreme lines of tones running vertically between white or black & this difference has to be regulated for different lighting accordingly. Viz., in studio the difference of lighting between horizontal & vertical is divided by the 7 vertical lines of tone. In sunshine the difference between full sunshine & the vertical is divided by the 7 vertical lines of tone, the instrument being used to transfer nature's hues to canvas accordingly.'

1 March 1908

SOME SITTERS FOR PORTRAITS BY E.F. WELLS

Lord Aberdare

Mrs Elfreda Bearman
Sir George and Lady Beaumont
Miss Marguerite Beauvais
Mrs Doris Bowyer
Lady Boyne and son
George Brann
Madame Bravet

Lady Romayne Cecil
Miss Charlton
Miss E.E. Cockett
Mrs E.E. Cox

Madelaine Davis and family
Trevor Davis
Mabel Delaforce's brothers
Monsieur Dessousier
Marchioness of Downshire
Mrs Edward Duke and daughters

Exeter family, *see* Cecil
Exmouth family, *see* Pellew
Lady Frances Exmouth

Mrs (D(?)) Farquarson
Mrs Agatha Fellowes
The Hon. Mrs Ailwyn Fellowes
Lord and Lady Forbes
Lady Muriel Fox-Strangeways

Miss Veronica Fullbrook-Leggatt

Sir William Gavin
Lady Archibald Grant
Lady Norton Griffiths
Lady Agatha Gurney and family

Sir Everard Hambro
Edward Hardisty
Mr and Mrs Robert Harvey
Lady Hastings
Miss Haviland
Josie Hay and family
Lieut.-Col. Hayley-Bell
The Hon. Mrs Mark Hovell
Mrs Georgina Howard
Francis Hughes
Anthony Hull
Mrs Hurndall-Waldron
   (Daphne Williams)

Lady Helen Ilchester

Mrs Aileen Kingsley Jarvis

Miss Mona Larmer
Mrs Constance Layard
Mrs Rose Leigh
Mrs Arbuthnot Leslie
The Hon. Kitty Liddell
Miss Sibyl Longman

Mrs Charlotte Ludicke
Dorothy and William Ludicke
Marlys Ludicke
Mr and Mrs Lushington

Father Vincent McNabb, OP
Sir Bernard Mallet
Lady Victor Mallet
Michael Marks (RAF)
Mrs Bessie Marriott
Alex Melrose
Mrs Laura Mengel-Byrne
Mrs J. Milne and son

Lady Newport

Peter Ormrod's family

Miss Lorna Pegg
Anne Pellew
Mary Rose Pellew
Mrs Violet Pellew
Mr G.(?) Platt
Major E.G. Pratt
Charles Pretzlik senior

Ravensworth family, *see* Liddell
Mrs Victor Riddle

Mrs Edwin Savitt
Lady Tilla Scarsdale

Mrs A. Seabright
Miss Margaret Sinclair
Miss Ethel Skardon
Lady Helen Stavordale
Dr Swayne

Revd H. Thursby
C.E. Trafford
Mr and Mrs Trefry
Mrs H.E. Tull

Mr Toshio Urabe

Madelaine Vandyck (Mrs Carruthers)
Sir William des Voeux

The Hon. Jane Walsh
Mrs Anne Wells (Anne Pellew)
Mrs Catharine Wells
Edward Francis Wells (four self-
    portraits)
Judith and Sylvia Wells (as girls)
Mrs Kay Ormsby Wells (and son)
Maud Wells
William Wells (as a boy)
William Howley Wells
Mrs William Howley Wells
Miss Daphne Williams of Scorrier
Mr and Mrs John Williams of
    Scorrier and family
J. Wyndham-Smith

E.F. WELLS'S EXHIBITS AT THE ROYAL ACADEMY

Date	Catalogue No.	Title
1897	657	*The Farm on the Hill*
1905	93	*Annie*
1907	201	*Maggie, Guy and Joan, Children of Peter Ormrod, Esq.*
	866	*Woodland*
1908	906	*A Wild Evening*
1911	772	*The Shower of Gold*
1912	207	*The Last Load*
1938	821	*Arosa, Switzerland*
1941	258	*Spring Woodland*

NOTES

Chapter One: Early Years

1 Theon Wilkinson, *Two Monsoons: European Influence in India as Represented in the Epitaphs & Monuments in Indian Cemeteries*, London, 1976, *passim*.
2 Quoted by Edward Francis Wells to his second wife, Katharine.
3 Miss E. Brown to Edward, 24 July 1897; E. Homan to Edward, 1 August 1897, and surviving press notices (provenance unidentified) of Edward's exhibition at Dorchester, 1901–2. These enquiries, including that of Mr Moreton, MP, were made after the *Farm on the Hill* was exhibited at the Royal Academy in 1897. See below in the text.
4 Mrs W.H. Wells to her son Edward, 10 November 1899, and Anne Pellew to Edward, 1 December 1899, both mentioning *Sandsfoot*.
5 Edward to Frank Bennett's father, 3 March 1900.
6 Edward to his mother, 8 February 1901.
7 The *Queen*, 30 April 1904. See also the *Ladies' Field* of 18 April 1904, the *Gentlewoman* of 23 April 1904, and *Vanity Fair* of April 28 1904.
8 *Gowan's Art Books*, Nos. 5 and 15, Glasgow, 1905 and 1908 respectively.
9 See the *Globe, 8 June 1904; Building News*, 11 June 1904; *Builder*, 18 February 1905; *Court Journal*, 8 April 1905; *Bazaar*, 21 July 1905 and 3 March 1906; *Daily Chronicle*, 27 February 1906; *Birmingham Post*, 27 February 1906; and the *Speaker*, 13 October 1906.
10 See the *Morning Post*, 18 April 1904; *Globe*, 31 October 1906; *Illustrated London News*, 3 November 1906; *Bazaar*, 6 November 1906; and *Ladies' Pictorial*, 9 November 1906.

Chapter Two: The Battle of Styles

1 Excerpts from Charles Alphonse du Fresnoy, *De Arte Graphica* ('Treatise on Art'), trans. Dr Pelles, Paris, 1668.
2 For further details, see Christopher Hussey, *The Life of Sir Edwin Lutyens*, 1950, p. 4, and Mary Lutyens, *Edwin Lutyens*, 1980, pp. 7, 45.
3 Charles Lutyens to Edward, 19 March, 1909.
4 W. Howley Wells, documents on true tone in painting, *c.* 1905.
5 C. Lutyens to Edward, *c.* March 1911.
6 J.B. Priestley, *The Edwardians*, 1970, p. 140.
7 C. Lutyens to Edward, 30 April, *c.* 1908.
8 W.H. Wells to Edward, 20 April 1902.
9 C. Lutyens to Edward, 24 March, 16 March, and 1 April 1908 respectively.
10 C. Lutyens to Edward, 14 March 1908.
11 C. Lutyens to Edward, 4 March and 11 May 1911.
12 C. Lutyens to Edward, 28 June 1911.
13 W.H. Wells, documents on true tone in painting, August 1905.
14 W.H. Wells to Edward, 24 March 1909.
15 W.H. Wells to Edward, 26 February 1902.
16 W.H. Wells to Edward, 7 March 1902. Howley Wells elaborates further his 'middle tint' theory as regards invisible rays and their effect on the eye. In strong daylight certain rays are invisible; but these become visible when an object is looked at in darkness, such as the

moon. He claims visible and invisible rays of light can be equalized to the eye from an object simply by looking at the least lit side through darkness, and thus the mystery of the middle tint seems solved through the existence of these more or less invisible rays. W.H. Wells, documents on true tone in painting, 9 August 1905.

17 W.H. Wells to Edward (paraphrased), 6 March 1902. In expressing keen interest in Edward's account of Lutyens's visit to the studio of a mutual friend named Vivian Rolt, Howley Wells wrote to his son: 'I don't see any way to throw objects edge to edge on a screen except on the principle of my box-sextant. With that instrument you can fix any object in the foreground, say, & after matching its tone on your painting, you can bring any other object in the landscape by the sextant against the first object already painted on your paper or canvas & so match its tone on your landscape.' The very next day he resumed the theme: 'Suppose a scale of tones made in various painting tints or colours, as in the case of the book of watercolour tints you sent me. With my box-sextant I can bring any object in the landscape, earth or sky on to & touching any tint in the book laid out in front of me in the same lighting as your canvas would be, & therefore we have matching tones on a screen as you wanted, & this can be done in nature's tone or in a slightly lower tone, I believe, as required. This seems to me to be a fair way to solve the difficulty as to tone in landscape. . . . The dictionary of tones that young [Fred] Lutyens talks of could be made in this way for all principal objects in landscape and kept for reference. Whether it is Lutyens's method or not, this seems to me by far the most practical way of matching tone that I have been able to think of.' W.H. Wells to Edward, 7 and 8 April 1902.

18 Despite the variations of sunshine effect, Howley Wells went on, and the consequent differing relations between the colours in a landscape, the same colours were still there as an underlying scheme of colour tone. They only rose or fell in tone according to the nature of the daylight. On a purely grey day, for example, skylight became the strongest light and there was a certain proportion between the vertical side of the box and the top side exposed to skylight; the backs of sheep on a purely grey day were an example. A similar rule as to skylight on a grey day applied to a studio lit by a top-light; while with a side-lit studio the matching was obtained directly on a nearly vertical canvas. An artist seeking nature's true colour tones could only do so by matching through a simple method which would give him the relation of colours on the three sides of the box in the proper key for painting them on canvas. W.H. Wells, documents on true tone in painting, *c*. August 1905.

19 Ibid. He continues thus: 'The shortening or lengthening of the tube found at the time according to the light of the day to bring skylight to full light determines the light on the canvas necessary to paint the effect. There is little difference between the proportions of illumination on the different sides of the box on either sunlight or grey days & therefore as objects in shadow do not change colour, only hue, they can be put into the picture at any time with the instrument. In studio portraits, one side of the box face being matched with every other side as well, half lights can be obtained with the instrument without the sitter being there if desired, & this of course applies to the rest of the picture. All sunlight effects are made possible in studio work by using yellow reflectors to reflect skylight instead of white reflectors.' W.H. Wells, documents on true tone in painting, *c*. August 1905. For further details on the instrument, see notes 21, 22, 25 and 30, and Appendix I.

20 Ibid.

21 For example, he enthused to Edward in early December 1906: 'The instrument seems very perfect, and I have through it learnt the complete theory of using the principle with absolute certainty, I think, both for grey days, all sunlight, and I hope even sunsets. I use no grey glass now, only ordinary mirrors for all ordinary effects and therefore get a very clean image as well as more perfect colours. . . . It also brings the matching together well and what it tells me about the changes in colour of the sky. . . .' Three days later he wrote: 'The perfected instrument I have now has led me much further on the principle. I now

know the true value between sky and earth lights. . . . All colours can be raised in painting a picture truly in tone. . . . In fact most subjects can be painted absolutely correctly in tone in nature's own colours unlowered, I believe. It is true that colours can only be matched in equal illuminations, but they can mathematically be brought up in colour on the canvas by my new instrument and method from the lowered colours to nature's own colours unlowered at all in tone in *many* subjects and very slightly lowered in *all* subjects.' He concluded his letter with the comment that all suspicion of blackness could now be eliminated, which had been the stumbling block in the process of 'lowering' colours. W.H. Wells to Edward, 3 and 6 December 1906.

22   W.H. Wells later mentioned these two men in connection with improvements to his instrument: 'I have been studying Hershell [sic] on light as well as Abney & have found the principle on which my tube brightens, or at least I have deduced the principle from study of the light waves & which I have no doubt in this, viz., that the waves of light from the object are increased in velocity from beating against the sides of the tube & are reflected more & more often backwards & forwards between the sides of the tube, according to its length & narrowness & consequently the intensity of the light is increased proportionally. Hence the longer & narrower a tube is, the greater the brightness. I have found this theory borne out in practice. My instrument is now set up with long, very narrow tubes of different lengths & the intensity of the light is so increased by the longer tube that I can match anything on the vertical. I can now reach the illumination of white in sunlight on the vertical easily. I can reach the sky close to the sun on the horizontal. . . . I can now reach all sunsets. I have also got rid of the troublesome reflections of the former instrument. The whole thing is becoming very perfect indeed. What the tube does is to take out colour due to the *lower* or vertical lighting on an object in proportion to its luminosity & so enable the change of colour due to the higher lighting being given to the object. It raises the tone by white light & so allows the warmer colour due to nature's higher lighting to be given on the lower lighting. No raising of the canvas by natural lights or lowering of the luminosity of the object can give this. Hence the brilliancy so obtained of the higher lightings on colours . . . Black in shadow should be taken as below the vertical to get the best results . . . & now that my tube will raise so much more, this becomes possible. Until you get the instrument to work with I should advise you to tip your canvas slightly for the vertical light towards you & match the darker colours by your palette in half light & your yellow & lighter colours in full light or nearly so & then transfer them to your tipped canvas instead of to a vertical canvas as before; but the instrument is the true thing.' W.H. Wells to Edward, spring 1909.

23   See Appendix I.

24   W.H. Wells, documents on true tone in painting, *c.* February 1908 and 1 March 1908. This meant in effect that as light was raised or lowered on colours, hue was taken out or increased in proportion to their luminosity as colours. Thus to represent the brilliance of the original colours when depicted in a lower key, one needed to lower them strictly in accordance with their respective luminosities, as otherwise brilliancy would be lost. This was more the case with colours bordering between the darker colours and orange or yellow, as, in lowering, the latter rays disappeared first. See also the final part of Appendix I.

25   W.H. Wells, documents on true tone in painting, 25 July 1908. Howley Wells stated that after comparing the colours so obtained witht he 'chess-board' base colours (i.e. all colours placed side by side, with the lowest hues of each colour on the bottom row in order to find their degree of illumination between white and black), all colours above black in shade had to be matched accordingly with the instrument in the following sequence: quarter power, half power, three-quarter power, full power.

26   W.H. Wells to Edward, 3 and 18 December 1906.

27   W.H. Wells to Edward, 19 January and 2 April 1908. Anne Pellew was Edward's future wife, of whom he had already painted more than one portrait.

28 W.H. Wells to Edward, 30 January 1908.

29 W.H. Wells to Edward, 22 February 1908. The letter continues thus: 'One knows they come into the next high illumination, viz., the instrument on half-light & that they are in tone still with the colours which were reached & matched in half-light. This one could not tell scientifically before the knowledge of the sunlight spectrum was known compared with shade spectrum. Also we now know that colors can be matched in groups, what we may call 'half-lights' of the different luminosity groups of colours. My idea is to make three such groups: 1) half-light, or instrument without tube, or the vertical for studio grey day & shade colours in sunshine; 2) half light in sunshine, or full tube on vertical for sunshine colours . . .; 3) higher half light, or instrument without tube, or the half light in sunshine for intenser colours near white. . . .' He ended by writing that he would continue his experiments, protecting his method by patent, but without inviting curious people to come in and ask a lot of silly questions demanding explanations.

30 W.H. Wells to Edward, 24 March 1908. The letter continues thus: 'There are two ways of matching, one way treating all lights & shades as colours with different luminosities & matching under the chess-board & tube method as before. The other way is to get the top lights truly with the instrument according to the respective luminosities of the colours & then grade downwards from the top colours in equal tones. Either way gives lustre colours perfectly . . . Matching all the top colours in the full light on them & from there stepping downwards in *equal* tones of shade will give tone but *not* lustre to all colours, unless the various luminosities of the top colours are allowed for. Nothing can be more lustre-like than the chess-board of colours & it proves conclusively where all top light colours come in.'

In a related letter of *c.* 1908, he continued his theme: 'The vertical in studio is the half-light, I am certain. It is always a right angle to full light & the position in which to place canvas in studio lighting. For Eosin dye & colours near it, viz., half-light colours, it is right to match them in half-light & transfer to the vertical – lighter colours in $\frac{3}{4}$ light, darker colours in $\frac{1}{4}$ light, all transferred to the vertical. You can't beat this till you have my instrument. It is perfect for all lightings on one & the same principle for all of them.' Claiming he had solved the principle of lustre as well as tone (two distinct things), he continued: 'I got some sunlight on my birthday & was enabled to solve a missing link required for perfection of the method & which after another close scrutiny of Abney & the theory of dark & light rays of the spectrum & especially as regards the absorption of light according to the luminosity of colours I wanted to try . . . I can now tell with a *certainty* what power to match every hue of nature individually by putting my chess-board of colours in full light whether in sunlight or otherwise.' Noting that the simplicity was splendid, he concluded that, although it was hard to know where one half-light power ended and the other began, any artist with a trained eye could resort to a half-lights method. He himself, seeking scientific accuracy, was very pleased with the results. First came tone, then lustre, while his chess-board of tints had proved a 'trump card' indeed.

31 Reference to the palette attachment is seen in the final part of the following letter, one of the last that Howley Wells wrote to his son and dated March 1909: 'So far you are right that for the colours first obtain true colour & then put it in the true lighting for my theory of luminosity, but white & its shades & black & its shades have to be treated in the same way. You must remember that every shade of white becomes a colour as regards its shades bearing a different black & white tone than the original white in light & each of these shades has to be transferred to canvas in its own black and white tone. To obtain white's shadow from the vertical for all its shades cannot be right, nor would it give sufficient depth of tone for the lighter shadow tints. We have to consider every kind of shade from the faintest shadow below white in full light to deep shades. I have found a means of comparing and transferring every shade of white from the lightest to the darkest as well as every shade of colours in the true black & white tone for each & every shade. All colours are matched in full light, brought to their common or true colour & transferred from it to the canvas according to the black & white tone or luminosity of every colour in all its

shades & all done with the palette, as regards portraits, & with palette and instrument as regards sunshine and sky. This is my advance on the former theory which was right as far as it went, but not perfect in manipulation. I expect we shall have to meet before you can use it as I require some colours graded into certain tones with my instrument as we graded black to white. This is essential & with that done & with my palette attachment you will find it all easy & I have no doubt of its correctness. Nor will you have when you see it. I doubt if I can well explain all to you without ocular demonstration but it is certainly important for you to know & practise it before you continue on portraits.'

For further information about the palette attachment see the end of 'Howley Wells's guidelines for adjusting colours to the vertical plane for studio lighting' in Appendix 1.

32 Arthur Schuster to W.H. Wells, Victoria Park, Manchester, 1 May 1909.
33 Vivian Rolt to Edward, 22 September 1922.
34 Years later the following typewritten comments were found among Edward's books, indicating his continuing interest in the Venetian 'mystery': 'The principle of the Venetians for light and shade was to use full black for full black in highlight, letting the shadow shift for itself, sometimes even putting local black darker in the light than shadow, to preserve the contrast. For colour: the paler and purer the colour, the more the Ventians will reinforce in the shadow and allow it to rise and fall in sympathy with the light.'

Chapter Three: Early Maturity
1   Anne Pellew to Mrs W.H. Wells, 22 November 1899.
2   Anne Pellew to Edward, 1 December 1899.
3   Mrs W.H. Wells to Edward, 2 May 1904.
4   W. Smith of Smith's Restaurant, 549 Fulham Road, 7 and 11 June 1904.
5   'Alastor', 57 Rostrever Road, Fulham, 3 December 1904.
6   The *World*, 7 November 1905; *Standard*, 9 November 1905; *Glasgow Herald*, 4 November 1905; see also *Nottingham Guardian*, 8 November 1905; and *Western Press* of Bristol, 10 November 1905. Some sixty years later, a dealer named Deliss really thought *Milking Time* was the work of an Old Master, Edward with tongue in cheek having signed it with deliberate obscurity on the back of the canvas.
7   The *Glasgow Herald* and *Daily News*, both 17 March 1906.
8   The *Glasgow Herald*, 10 October 1906; *Daily News, October 15 1906; Western Press*, 16 October 1906; and *Art Journal*, December 1906.
9   The *Queen*, 1 April 1905; *Times*, 5 May 1907; and *Glasgow Herald*, 11 May 1907.
10 Maud to Edward, 27 April 1907.
11 Edward painted Major and Mrs John Williams of Scorrier, and their children John, George, Stephen and Mary, in 1907. He painted their granddaughter Daphne in the winter of 1936/7 ('the girl with the apple'). During his first visit he also painted sea views of Cornwall.
12 Edward to Anne Pellew, *c*. July 1907.
13 W.H. Wells to Edward, 16 July 1909.
14 Maud to Edward and Anne, 4 January 1910.
15 Revd Harvey W.G. Thursby (The Rectory, Bergh Apton, Norwich) to Edward, *c*. 15 June 1910.
16 The *Huddersfield Chronicle* and *Huddersfield Examiner*, both 29 August 1912.
17 *In a Chelsea Garden* was warmly recommended by Mr Ronald Alley, Keeper of the Modern Collection at the Tate Gallery, many years later, and was submitted to the committee, where it apparently just failed to win an affirmative vote.
18 In the cartoon two women look at the painting through lorgnettes and one exclaims, 'La Burn 'Em!', *Punch*, *c*. May 1911. But compare with positive reviews (below in text) in the *Academy*, 13 May 1911, and *View*, 20 May 1911.

19 The *Daily Express* of Dublin, 2 March 1914.
20 Quoted by Charles Moreau-Vauthier in his *The Technique of Painting*, London, 1912, p. 206. A similar fate befell Edward's *Kay Under a Yellow Umbrella* many years later when a restorer altered the face.

Chapter Four: The First World War and Tragedy
 1 Mrs W.H. Wells to Edward, 14 November 1916.
 2 Mrs W.H. Wells to Edward, 14, 23 and 29 November 1916.
 3 Mrs W.H. Wells to Edward, 2 January 1917.
 4 Mrs W.H. Wells to Edward, 8, 10 and 16 May 1917.
 5 Edward to Anne at Wimbledon, as soldier No. 23915, from Army Post Office 25, 8 July *c*. 1917 (the year not given).
 6 Edward to Anne, 26 August *c*. 1917.
 7 Edward to Anne, 7 February *c*. 1919.
 8 Ibid.
 9 Stephanie Cayley to Edward, 8 July 1922.
10 Sibyl Longman to Edward, 14 May 1922.
11 Edward to his mother, 23 September 1923.
12 Edward to Anne, 19 September 1923.
13 Edward to Anne, 22 September 1923.
14 Edward to Anne, 23 September 1923.
15 Edward to Anne, 26 September 1923.
16 For example, his letter to his mother of 28 October 1923.
17 Ibid.
18 Edward to his mother, 4 November 1923.

Chapter Five: The Years Between
 1 Edward to Anne, 26 September 1923.
 2 Lord Forbes to Edward, 4 August 1925.
 3 Trevelyan Turner to Edward, 21 January 1926.
 4 For example, Mrs Robert Harvey proposed fifty guineas for a portrait, arranged by Trevelyan Turner, in a letter to Edward of 30 November 1927.
 5 Constance Layard to Edward, *c*. 1929.
 6 Madelaine Davis to Edward, *c*. 1933. Edward painted a Mr Trevor Davis in about 1930, who may have been a relation.
 7 Mrs Josie Hay to Edward, 1 November 1930.
 8 Examples were Edward's commissions from Captain T. Colville and H.D. Colville (of Cheltenham and Salop respectively) for a portrait of their father, R.N. Colville, around 1931; and those from Sir Campbell Stuart between 1929 and 1933. A Canadian director of *The Times*, the last named was assistant military attaché at the British embassy in Washington DC in 1917, a deputy-director of the propaganda campaign in enemy countries, and subsequently on the council of the Royal Institute for Foreign Affairs. Some of Edward's commissions may also have been merely to make copies. J. Hoyle, Chelsea Arts Club secretary in 1926, mentions a 'varnishing cheque' in a letter to Edward, along with a portrait which may fall into any category.
 9 Mrs W.H. Wells to Edward, 7 July 1931.
10 Ingrid Horst to the author, *c*. 1988, concerning this painting of 1934.
11 Some of these may be from before 1920. Among Edward's exhibitions in the 1920s, it is believed (not verified) that one was given at the Walker Art Gallery in Liverpool.

Chapter Six: A New Life Begins
 1 Edward to Katharine, Dorset, 31 July 1935.
 2 Edward to Katherine, 1935.

3 See also Belinda Morse, *John Hanson Walker*, Gloucester, 1987, p. 61.
4 Edward Irving, Lord Exmouth, to Edward, 12 July 1936; Georgina Howard to Edward, 13 July 1937.
5 The *Times*, 18 June 1937; *Morning Post*, 19 June 1937; *Birmingham Post*, 28 June 1937; *Hampstead and Highgate Express*, *c.* 28 June 1937; *Walker's Monthly*, June 1937 and November 1938; and *Hampstead and Highgate Express*(?), *c.* 25 November 1938.

Chapter Seven: The Second World War and Triumph
1 Harold Ludicke to Edward, 31 July 1940.
2 Toshio Urabe to Katharine, 15 May 1989 (and previous correspondence), recalling his portrait by Edward of *c.* 30 November to early December 1941.
3 Pownoll, Lord Exmouth, to Edward, 23 September 1942, and *c.* January 1943.
4 G.P. Williams of Scorrier to Edward, 29 November 1944.
5 A case in point is that of Lt.-Col. Hayley Bell, done in earlier months.
6 Anne Walsh to Edward about the portrait of her daughter the Hon. Jane Walsh, 10 April 1947.

Chapter Eight: The Watch That Didn't Stop
1 Katharine took down Edward's comments verbatim, but they are here given in reported speech with some minor inversions to enhance the points made.
2 A.F.H. Lindner to Edward, 9 November 1949.
3 Further purchasers and visitors, possibly recalling Edward's Sloane Street gallery, included: Gwen Ashenford; John Cottrell; Hubert Dougall; J.W. Evans; Philip Hartley; Dorothy Ludicke; Joan MacLeod; Vera Ramsden; Joan Saul; John Way; and Sibyl Weir.
4 Sir William Gavin to Edward, 10 June 1951.

Chapter Nine: Postscript in Wessex and Westphalia
1 Other purchasers included: F.B. Clifford (who probably attended the Yeovil exhibition); Martin Fisher (the one at Bath); Chris Gaskell (Taunton); R. Hayne (Weymouth); Beryl Heard of Wales (Winchester?); David Wallis of Loughton; and Peter Watson of Kingsbridge. Maurice Bowyer, Daphne Thomas and Gerald de Boynville, mentioned previously, possibly continued their contacts when Katharine exhibited in London.
2 Val Orrin, *Western Gazette*, *c.* 15 November 1954.
3 A.C.B., *Western Gazette*, 21 June 1957.

Chapter Ten: Appraisal
1 Margaret Sinclair to Katharine, undated, *c.* 1952.
2 Quoted in *Bazaar*, 6 November 1906.

Appendix I: The 'Venetian Secret' and 'True-tone Painting'
1 W.H. Wells, documents on true tone in painting, 30 June 1907.
2 Ibid. Thus, for example, with cobalt, blue-green, vermillion, brown (paper), and emerald green, given fairly low luminosity value in relation to white at a hundred (Abney's table), Howley Wells would accord a luminosity power of two to these colours. Eosin dye, orange, and chrome yellow, being of higher value, would each earn two and a half. White, being given a hundred, would earn the highest power at three. Ultramarine blue at the opposite end of the scale earned only one. This latter colour in terms of instrument use was represented by simply double-reflecting both object and canvas. Colours of group two were represented by the instrument being used without any tube and double-reflecting the object only. Colours of group two and a half required the instrument's short tube, double-reflecting the object only; while white, with the power of three required the instrument's long tube, likewise double-reflecting the object only.
3 Ibid.

4   W.H. Wells, documents on true tone in painting, *c.* February 1908. An example of these 'powers' can be seen with studio light vertical. Representing the lighting in which a picture is painted, this is the plane of lighting on which all nature's colours have to be adjusted so as to preserve the same differences of black and white tones between them, as in nature. And if colours are painted, as with landscapes, on the vertical out of doors, an adjustment has to be made to bring them to the studio vertical lighting. This studio vertical is to full light as follows: to studio full light, *one* power below; to out-of-doors full light, *two* powers below; to sunlight full light, *three* below.

BIBLIOGRAPHY

PRIMARY SOURCES

Miscellaneous letters to and from Edward Francis Wells
Wells, Edward Francis, Annotations to unnumbered pages found in his notes of *De Arte Graphica* ('Treatise on Art') by Charles Alphonse du Fresnoy (translated by Dr Pelles; Paris, 1668)
———, Correspondence with his first wife, Anne (Pellew)
———, Correspondence with his mother, Mrs W.H. Wells
———, Correspondence with his second wife, Katherine (Stather Dunn)
———, Diary
———, Notes
———, 'Views on other artists'
Wells, Maud, Letters to her brother, Edward Francis Wells
Wells, William Howley, Documents on true tone in painting
———, Letters to his son, Edward Francis Wells

CONTEMPORARY SOURCES

(In locating contemporary reviews I have been assisted by Durrant's Press Cuttings, the General Press Cutting Association and the International Press Cutting Bureau; for specific issues see Notes and Index)
Academy
Art Journal
Bazaar Exchange & Mart
Birmingham Post
Builder
Building News
Court Journal
Daily Chronicle
Daily Express (of Dublin)
Daily Graphic
Daily News
Dorchester County Chronicle
Dorset Evening Echo
Evening Standard
Gentlewoman
Glasgow Herald
Globe
Gowan's Art Books
Hampstead and Highgate Express
Huddersfield Chronicle
Huddersfield Examiner

Illustrated London News
Ladies' Field
Ladies' Pictorial
Morning Post
Nottingham Guardian
Pulman's Weekly
Punch
Queen
Speaker
Standard
Throne
Times
Vanity Fair
View
Walker's Monthly
Western Gazette
Western Press
World

SECONDARY SOURCES

Brophy, J. *The Human Face*, G.G. Harrap, 1945
Gaunt, William, *The Impressionists*, Thames & Hudson, 1970
Gwynne-Jones, A., *Portrait Painters*, Phoenix House, 1950
Hillier, Bevis, *The Style of the Century, 1900–1980*, The Herbert Press, 1982
Hussey, Christopher, *The Life of Sir Edwin Lutyens*, Charles Scribner's, New York, 1950
Hutchinson, Sidney, *History of the Royal Academy, 1768–1968*, Chapman & Hall, 1968
Hynes, Samuel, *The Edwardian Turn of Mind*, Princeton University Press, 1968
Lutyens, Mary, *Edwin Lutyens*, John Murray, 1980
Moreau-Vauthier, Charles, *The Technique of Painting*, Heinemann, 1912
Morse, Belinda, *John Hanson Walker*, Alan Sutton, Stroud, 1987
Nowell-Smith, Simon, *Edwardian England*, Oxford University Press, 1964
Piper, David, *The English Face*, Thames & Hudson, 1957
Priestley, J.B., *The Edwardians*, Sphere Books, 1970
Sackville-West V., *The Edwardians*, The Hogarth Press, 1930
Wilkinson, Theon Charles, *Two Monsoons: European Influence in India, as Represented in the Epitaphs & Monuments in Indian Cemeteries*, Duckworth, 1976
Wilson, Simon, *British Art from Holbein to the Present Day*, Tate Gallery and Bodley Head, 1979

INDEX

For reference to E.F. Wells's portraits, see under the respective patron's name; for titles of his paintings, including scenes in general, see under Wells, Edward Francis, works mentioned.